ANGUS - CULTURAL SERVICES

3 8046 00696

C000132871

25 WAL

BRECHIN

This book is to be returned on or
before the last date stamped below.

B

2 2 JUN 2000

2 9 JUL 2000
1 9 MAY 2005

2 4 NOV 2005

3 0 MAR 2009

1 4 NOV 2012

ANGUS COUNCIL
CULTURAL SERVICES
WITHDRAWN
FROM STOCK

Angus Council

CULTURAL SERVICES
C APR 2000

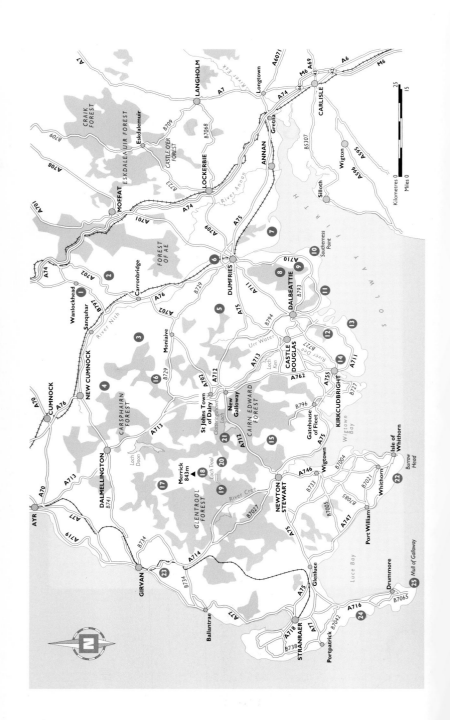

25 WALKS

DUMFRIES AND GALLOWAY

Tom Prentice

Series Editor: Roger Smith

MERCAT PRESS

© Mercat Press 1999

First published 1995

This revised edition published 1999

ISBN 1 873644 91 4

Acknowledgements

The publisher acknowledges with thanks the valuable assistance given by Dumfries and Galloway Enterprise, Dumfries and Galloway Area Tourist Board, Dumfries and Galloway Regional Council, Department of Physical Planning and Scottish Natural Heritage South West Region in the preparation of this guide and for the supply of additional transparencies.

The publisher's thanks are due to Tom Prentice, the author, for access to and use of transparencies throughout the book.

Maps prepared by HMSO Cartographic Centre.

Printed in China through World Print Ltd.

CONTENTS

USEFUL INFORMATION

The length of each walk is given in kilometres and miles, but within the text measurements are metric for simplicity. The walks are described in detail and are supported by accompanying maps (study them before you start the walk), so there is little likelihood of getting lost, but if you want a back-up you will find the 1:25 000 Pathfinder Ordnance Survey maps on sale locally.

Every care has been taken to make the descriptions and maps as accurate as possible, but the author and publishers can accept no responsibility for errors, however caused. The countryside is always changing and there will inevitably be alterations to some aspects of these walks as time goes by. The publishers and author would be happy to receive comments and suggested alterations for future editions of the book.

Transport
The two main bus companies for public transport are Western Buses (01387 253496) and MacEwan's Coaches (01387 710357).
For rail timetables contact the National Rail Enquiry Service (0345 484950)

Tourist Information
Dumfries and Galloway Tourist Board, Campbell House, 64 Whitesands, Dumfries DG1 2RS (01387 253862) for general enquiries. Website: *www.galloway.co.uk*

Tourist Information Centres
Open all year:
Dumfries (01387 253862).
Stranraer, Harbour Street (01776 702595).

Open Apr.-Oct.:
Castle Douglas, Markethill (01556 502611).
Gatehouse of Fleet, car park (01557 814212).
Gretna Green (01461 337834)
Kirkcudbright, Harbour Square (01557 330494).
Moffat, Churchgate (01683 220620)
Newton Stewart, Dashwood Square (01671 402431).

Any brochure available at the above tourist offices can be sent to you by phoning 01426 976731 (calls charged at local rate).

METRIC MEASUREMENTS

At the beginning of each walk, the distance is given in miles and kilometres. Within the text, all measurements are metric for simplicity (and indeed our Ordnance Survey maps are now all metric). However, it was felt that a conversion table might be useful to those readers who, like the author, still tend to think in Imperial terms.

The basic statistic to remember is that one kilometre is five-eighths of a mile. Half a mile is equivalent to 800 metres and a quarter-mile is 400 metres. Below that distance, yards and metres are little different in practical terms.

km	miles
1	0.625
1.6	1
2	1.25
3	1.875
3.2	2
4	2.5
4.8	3
5	3.125
6	3.75
6.4	4
7	4.375
8	5
9	5.625
10	6.25
16	10

All the tourist information centres are very well organised and have wide details of local transport, accommodation, plus a bookshop selling guides, books of local interest and maps.

For the Girvan area, contact the Ayrshire Tourist Board on 01465 714950.

Other Useful Addresses

Dumfries & Galloway Council, Senior Countryside Ranger, Planning and Environmental Consultancy Group, Environment and Infrastructure, Rae Street, Dumfries DG1 2JD (01387 260184).

A wide variety of ranger-led walks are organised throughout the Dumfries and Galloway area from May to October and are publicised in a booklet available from Dumfries and Galloway Council at the above address, or from tourist information centres.

Forest Enterprise offices are found at: Ae (01387 860247); Castle Douglas (01556 503626); and Galloway (01671 402420).

Forest Enterprise publish a number of leaflets detailing walks in various areas. Details from the Forest Enterprise numbers listed above or from: Forestry Commission, 55/57 Moffat Road, Dumfries DO1 1NP (01387 272440); Ae Forest District, Ae Village, Dumfries DG1 1QB (01387 286247). You may also find these leaflets in tourist information centres.

Wilson Ogilvie of Dumfries Bridgend Tourist Services organises regular walks round the town (01387 264267).

Buccleuch Estates Visitor Services, Drumlanrig Castle, Thornhill, Dumfriesshire DG3 4AQ (01848 331555).

Hoddam and Kinmount Estates: Estate Office (01576 300244).

The National Trust for Scotland, Regional Office, Northgate House, 32 Northgate, Peebles EH45 8RS (01721 722502).

Threave School of Horticulture, Castle Douglas DG7 1RX (01556 502575).

Scottish Natural Heritage, Dumfries and Galloway Area Office, Carmont House, The Crichton, Bankhead Road, Dumfries DG1 4ZF (01387 247010).

Scottish Wildlife Trust, Dumfries Ranger Team (01387 248419).

Wildfowl and Wetlands Trust, Eastpark Farm, Caerlaverock, Dumfries DG1 4R5 (01387 770200). The Dumfriesshire Bat Group can be contacted at the same address.

Weather

Up-to-date forecasts for South-West Scotland can be obtained on Weather Check (0990 100844).

INTRODUCTION

The Dumfries and Galloway region of Scotland has considerable charms, as I hope you will discover for yourself during the course of following the walks in this book.

In terms of landscape, the area seems to have everything; small but rugged granite mountains rising above fertile lowlands and a dramatic indented coastline of long sandy beaches and towering cliffs. Prosperous communities have lived here since the Stone Age, and the area is rich in chambered tombs and standing stones. In the 5th century AD, St Ninian built Scotland's first Christian church on the Solway Coast near Whithorn, an area which continues to be of great archaeological interest. Over the years religion played a major part in the region's development, and the remains of several large abbeys can also be found.

It was in south-west Scotland that Robert the Bruce started his campaign for Scottish independence in the early 14th century, fighting and winning battles round Glen Trool, before going on to final victory at Bannockburn near Stirling. For many years the area was fought over by the Scots and English, which accounts for a number of impressive castles.

More recent history includes the poet Robert Burns, who lived the final five years of his short life in Dumfries and is buried there. Prior to and during the second war the area was used for pilot training and many of the hills are littered with crashed planes. The screech of a low-flying jet remains a frequent occurrence.

Although the hills included in this book are not very high, the walking is quite rough and a sturdy pair of boots are recommended. Start with something more straightforward like Criffel before venturing onto the likes of Merrick, and remember that all these hills should be treated with respect. No one should head out onto the hills in poor weather without a map and compass (and competence in their use) and suitable clothing.

The majority of the walks are off-road and range from 6 to 16 km in length. Although most are in the Dumfries and Galloway area, the eagle- eyed will notice these boundaries have been stretched a little to the west and north! All the walks are suitable for families with children, although it should be noted that the hillwalks round Glen Trool are rough underfoot and quite tiring for the modest distances and heights involved.

In general the weather in the south-west is a lot drier than the rest of Scotland's west coast and the coastal areas get a lot of sun during the summer. The driest months are often April to June, with July and August likely to be wetter. The autumn and winter months can also be very pleasant, although a lot of snow can fall on the hills in a cold winter.

Hopefully the variety of landscape and walking in this beautiful, easily accessible, but not over-visited part of Scotland will inspire you to return again and again to explore beyond the walks in this book.

TOM PRENTICE

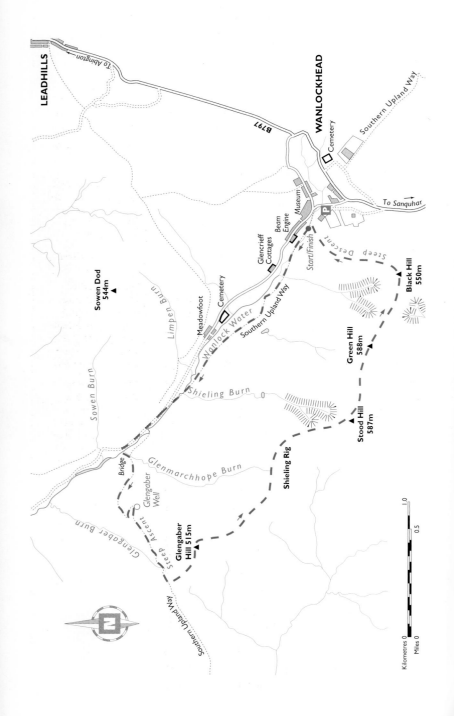

LEADHILLS

To Abington

WANLOCKHEAD

B797

Cemetery

Southern Upland Way

To Sanquhar

Museum

Beam Engine

Glencrieff Cottages

Start/Finish

Steep Descent

Black Hill 550m

Meadowfoot

Cemetery

Wanlock Water

Sowen Dod 544m

Limpen Burn

Southern Upland Way

Green Hill 588m

Sowen Burn

Shieling Burn

Stood Hill 587m

Glenmarchhope Burn

Bridge

Shieling Rig

Glengaber Well

Steep Ascent

Glengaber Burn

Glengaber Hill 515m

Southern Upland Way

N

Kilometres 0   0.5   1.0
Miles 0

WANLOCKHEAD

Passing through Clydesdale and Annandale, whether on the M74 or by train, you cannot help being uplifted by the beauty of the rural setting; heather and sheep covered hillsides, rivers meandering through flat fertile fields. This is the green heart of Scotland's border region at its finest.

Yet within a short distance is an altogether harsher industrial landscape of dark slagheaps and rusting mine machinery in a rugged upland environment. At 422 m, Wanlockhead is the highest village in Scotland and with the neighbouring village of Leadhills has been the centre of a leadmining industry since the 17th century, although lead was mined in the area as early as the 13th century.

It was gold retrieved from the area's alluvial gravel that made the area famous. This gold went into coins for the Scottish treasury in the 1540s and was incorporated into the Scottish regalia. Mining at that time was an international business with Dutch, German, French, Flemish and English experts trying their luck. Some of these opencast mines can still be seen at the head of the Longcleuch Burn below Wellgrain Dod, north of Leadhills, and on the eastern flanks of Wool Law and Broad Law.

However, it was the deep mining of lead and zinc that really boosted and sustained the area until the last mines closed in the late 1950s. Leadhills was developed by the Hopetoun family in the 17th century, although most of what can be seen nowadays is from an intensive period of development in the 18th and 19th centuries. Mining at Wanlockhead began a little later and the village retains a number of sites of considerable interest, some of which can be visited in the course of the walk.

The car-park by the Wanlockhead Museum Trust's Museum of Leadmining gives the best starting point. The museum has a shop, restaurant, toilets and

INFORMATION

Distance: 7 km (4½ miles).

Start and Finish: Wanlockhead Museum of Leadmining car-park.

Terrain: The hills can be quite rough underfoot and adequate footwear is recommended, as are waterproofs and a map and compass in poor weather.

Map: OS Landranger Sheet 71.

Refreshments: *Wanlockhead Museum of Leadmining* (daily, Apr-Oct, 1100–1630, Jul-Aug 1000–1630) has a shop, tea room, toilets and a restaurant.

Other Activities: The museum has various displays and can organise a visit down a mine and to period cottages.

displays detailing the history of the area. Visits to various mines can also be arranged.

Across the road from the car-park is a sign for the Southern Upland Way. Follow the path, passing the remains of the old Pate's Knowe smelt mill on the left and then the more modern New Glencrieff Mine with its danger signs and keep-out notices. This mine was the last to be closed in the late 1950s. The large slagheap in the middle is very pointed, almost like a miniature mountain.

Wanlockhead from the Southern Upland Way to the south.

On the right, on the other side of the Wanlock Water you can see an old beam engine, now in the care of Historic Scotland. Keeping mines drained was always a problem and although steam engines were efficient, coal was expensive. This beam pumping engine is water-powered via a simple bucket and cistern system, the only remaining example in Scotland. A little further down on the right is the village graveyard containing the stones of a number of miners killed in accidents.

The path soon turns into a track as you move out of the industrial landscape. After about 25 minutes it's best to cross over the Wanlock Water to a track, as the route down on the left, although quite possible, is wet and muddy. The track on the right continues down to a new girder bridge on the left with a Southern Upland Way signpost. On the right is the remains of an old smelt mill, one of the best preserved sites in the area. Stripped of vegetation from years of lead fumes, the landscape has a desolate moonscape appearance.

Cross over the bridge and the stile and follow the track to skirt Glengaber Hill on the right. Contour round the side of the hill on a good wide track via various bends, until you pass the top of a gully where a burn runs down to join Wanlock Water. It's worth stopping

Approaching Stood Hill.

for a moment for the view back to the rounded top of Sowen Dod and the solitary white house of Duntercleuch. Continue on the track, rising as you go until you arrive at the open col below Glengaber Hill on the left.

Leave the Southern Upland Way, go up on the left, cross through a gate and continue up and over the hill to a col and quite a steep climb up the other side. Some fine views are possible from here down towards Wanlockhead on the left. Follow the fence until the way is barred by another fence which can be crossed via a gate on the left. The fence then leads down left for about 90 m to another gate. From the top of Stood Hill you can see Lowther Hill straight ahead with its pylons and 'golf balls' of the Civil Aviation Authority radar station.

From the top of Stood Hill drop down, heading towards Lowther Hill, and follow a fence to the col between Stood Hill and Black Hill above the road. Go through the gap in the fence and up onto Black Hill.

Looking down on to Wanlockhead from Black Hill.

From here there is an extensive view over Wanlockhead and down on the right towards the Mennock Pass. The broad spur overlooking Wanlockhead can now be descended, past wooden and earthen grouse shooting butts to the road.

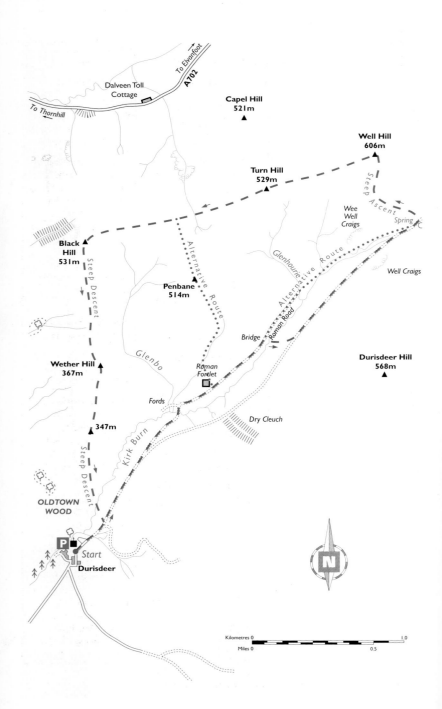

To Elvanfoot

A702

Dalveen Toll
Cottage

To Thornhill

Capel Hill
521m
▲

Well Hill
606m
▲

Turn Hill
529m
▲

Steep Ascent

Wee
Well
Craigs

Spring

Black
Hill
531m
▲

Steep Descent

Alternative Route

Glenhourie Route

Well Craigs

Penbane
514m
▲

Alternative Route

Roman Road

Bridge

Durisdeer Hill
568m
▲

Wether Hill
367m
▲

Glenbo

Roman
Fordlet

▲ 347m

Fords

Dry Cleuch

Steep Descent

Kirk Burn

OLDTOWN
WOOD

P

Start
Durisdeer

N

Kilometres 0   1.0

Miles 0   0.5

DURISDEER AND WELL HILL

This walk round the small hills north of Durisdeer village is notable for glimpses into quite different periods of Scottish history.

A sundial over the south entrance to the church at Durisdeer dates it at 1699, and the church is surprisingly large for such a small village. However, a walk round to the back of the building goes some way to explaining this by revealing a burial aisle with a marble floor and a large marble canopy (baldachin) supported by four ornate columns.

This edifice covers the entrance to the burial vault of the 1st Duke of Queensberry, designed by the architect James Smith. The first Duke, who died in 1695, is noted for starting the building of Drumlanrig Castle, which can usually be seen from the top of Black Hill on the walk.

On the wall is a marble mural carved in 1712 by Anglo-Dutch sculptor John van Nost to commemorate James Douglas, the 2nd Duke, and his wife Mary. Known as the 'Union Duke' for his active role in the 1707 Treaty of Union, the 2nd Duke died in 1717.

At the front of the church is a table-tomb to Covenanter Daniel McMichael, executed in 1685, and the graveyard contains a headstone carved with an effigy of a mason holding a mell and chisel to mark the grave of William Lukup, Master of Works during the

INFORMATION

Distance: 9 km (5½ miles).

Start and Finish: Durisdeer village. Park near the war memorial outside the church.

Terrain: Good tracks and open hillside. These hills are small and the going is not too rough, but the route is steep in places and walking boots are recommended. Waterproofs and a map and compass are advised in poor weather.

Map: OS Landranger sheet 78, Nithsdale and Annandale.

Refreshments: Full facilities in Sanquhar.

Other Activities: The 14th century ruin of *Morton Castle* (GR 874999) off the A702 south-east of Durisdeer is well worth visiting.

Opening Hours: *Drumlanrig Castle* nearby dates from the late 1600s and is the stately home of the Earls of Queensberry. It is open to the public from the first Saturday in May to the last Monday in August, Mon. to Sat. 1100–1600, Sunday 1200–1600.

Looking towards Durisdeer with Black Hill on the left and Penbane in the centre.

The mausoleum of the Duke and Duchess of Queensbery in Durisdeer Church.

building of Drumlanrig Castle, who died in 1685. (See Walk 19, Loch Trool, for more information on the Covenanters.) A tall timber spire which used to adorn the central tower was removed in the 19th century.

From the church, follow the road up on the right past a couple of cottages to a gate where it turns into a track. From here on you are on a Roman road, a branch from the main route north that followed the rough line of today's A74. Known as the Well Path, the road follows the Kirk Burn to the saddle below Well Hill and then follows the Potrail Water and the course of the modern A702 to join the 'main' Roman road and the A74 at Elvanfoot, where there is the site of a Roman camp. This route was also used in medieval times, forming one of the overland routes to the shrine of St Ninian at Whithorn.

The road itself is hard to distinguish from a well-laid farm track, but there is no mistaking the foundations of the fortlet which commands an impressive view down the glen from the base of Benbane hill. The road itself may have been in operation in the Flavian era, AD85 to c.105, but the fortlet is one of a number established during the Antonine period after AD142 to house detachments from main forts as a means of local control.

To view the fortlet, follow the track to the first gate on the left-hand side. Go through this and take a lower track (the Roman road) which is much more grassy and overgrown. The track leads through a field, crosses the Kirk Burn and then turns right and ascends the hillside, not as clearly now. The fortlet consists of a single 9 m thick rampart with an outer ditch and counterscarp bank. Excavation inside revealed the remains of timber structures.

Go through another two gates and continue on the track. From here it is possible to continue on the Roman road, but it turns into an indistinct path through marshy ground before it rises to the col below Well Hill, so you return to the right-hand track. To do this descend on the right after the second gate and cross a stile. A short, rough pull up the other side regains the main track which can be followed to the col.

At the col, pass through a gate and take the obvious right to left diagonal path up Well Hill, starting to the left of a wall. Where the path ends on the shoulder, go straight up the steep rabbit-warrened slope, with fine views to Penbane Hill and Cairnsmore of Carsphairn in the distance, to a wall which is followed up and right to the summit.

The summit itself has little interest, but the views are fine and the radio masts and 'golf ball' aerials on Lowther Hill are clearly visible. At the summit it's worth crossing over the wall and the fence on the left, but take care as the fence can be electrified.

Descend beside the wall and the fence towards Black Hill in the distance. The next little hill is soon crossed and you descend to the col between Penbane Hill and Black Hill, passing through a gate just below the col, where the fence starts to rise up Black Hill.

A number of choices are possible from this col. You can go up Penbane Hill on the left and then descend to the Roman fortlet, or continue up Black Hill and descend the long ridge back to Durisdeer. From the col the A702 can be seen winding through 'the lang glen' of the Dalveen Pass below.

The trig point on Black Hill's summit gives fine views of solitary Criffel to the south and the main Galloway hills, Carsphairn, Merrick and the Rhinns of Kells to the west. Surrounded by forest, straight ahead in the valley below, is the imposing Drumlanrig Castle. The castle is open to the public, although its hours are limited.

The flanks of Well Hill with Penbane and Nithsdale in the distance.

From the summit descend the hillside to a fence. Pass through it at a gate and go over the final small hill to the burn. Cross it and the field beyond to a gate which gives access to the main track near its start.

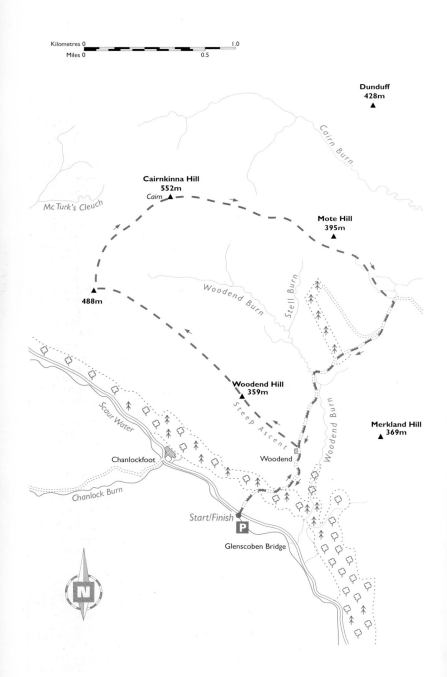

Kilometres 0   1.0
Miles 0   0.5

Dunduff
428m
▲

Cairn Burn

Cairnkinna Hill
552m
Cairn ▲

McTurk's Cleuch

Mote Hill
395m
▲

Woodend Burn

Stell Burn

▲
488m

Woodend Hill
359m
▲

Steep Ascent

Woodend Burn

Merkland Hill
369m
▲

Scaur Water

Chanlockfoot

Woodend

Chanlock Burn

Start/Finish
P

Glenscoben Bridge

N

CAIRNKINNA

South-west of the Lowther Hills, a series of glens run north-west into the upland area north of the village of Moniavie and east of Cairnsmore of Carsphairn. The most northerly of these glens is that of the Scaur Water, followed in part by the Southern Upland Way after its climb to the summit of Benbrack (Walk 16).

This is a beautiful area, lower in altitude and softer in landscape than the hills and glens of the Lowther Hills to the north. The Scaur Water is surrounded for much of its route down the glen by birch forest, and the lower section of the glen has a pleasant, relaxing atmosphere. Higher up the glen the trees peter out, but it does not become less picturesque as a result.

Many hours can be spent wandering the country lanes and the banks of the Scaur Water in the lower glen, but for a better view of the area a short walk up Cairnkinna is well worth the effort. The hill is particularly noteworthy for the massive, although partially demolished, well-built cairn that crowns its summit, something more at home on the summit of Ben Nevis or Scafell, than such a lowly hill as this. Who put in the effort and when, and why they bothered is not known, but it's no less worthy of our admiration for this.

INFORMATION

Distance: 7km (4½ miles).

Start and Finish: At the start of the Woodend track. From Thornhill on the A76, take A702 west through Penpont, cross the Scaur Water and then turn right. Follow this narrow road for 7 km and turn left at the junction. Continue up the glen for about 2 km and look for a gate on the right from which a track crosses a grassy field and into woods. This is about 1.5 km past Woodside at GR795997. There's limited parking at a field entrance on the left-hand side beside the tree-screened river. Make particularly sure you do not obscure any of the field gates.

Terrain: The higher ground can be a bit rough and boggy, although there are reasonable tracks. The end of the walk goes through sheep fields and the route should be avoided in the lambing season (March to May), or very great care taken. Dogs should not be taken on this walk.

Map: OS Landranger Sheet 78, Nithsdale.

Refreshments: None.

Opening Hours: *Drumlanrig Castle* nearby dates from the late 1600s and is the stately home of the Earls of Queensberry. It is open to the public from the first Saturday in May to the last Monday in August, Mon. to Sat. 1100–1600, Sunday 1200–1600.

Solitary hawthorn in the valley of the Scaur Water with the flanks of Chanlock Rig and Craigdasher on the left.

The Scaur Water with the flanks of Chanlock Rig and Craigdasher on the left.

Cairnkinna is also interesting for the marked change in landscape as you rise in altitude. Green, wooded and grassy at first, the terrain soon turns to more rugged tussocky grass above the 350 metre contour.

The walk starts by following the track (GR 795997) between Woodside and Chanlockfoot, to the ruined farm at Woodend. Go through the gate on the right, cross the field to another gate and enter the wood. The wood soon ends and the track goes up through open fields towards Woodend. This is a good example of a farmhouse and cattle byre rolled into one. The building probably hasn't been unoccupied long, the window frames are still intact although the glass has gone and there is plaster and panelling on the walls, but the elements are already taking their toll and the roof is beginning to deteriorate. The only inhabitants seem to be a congregation of pigeons in the rafters.

The best way onto the hillside is to return to the gable end facing down the glen, turn left and follow the fence to a gate which leads out onto the broad ridge ascending the hillside. The route seems to be a little easier over to the left and you will get a good view down the glen. In summer much of this area is covered with rabbits and the bracken will need a little gentle bushwhacking.

As you rise above Woodend, various tracks appear which are used by the farm to supply feed to sheep and cattle on the hillside, and these can be followed on and off for much of the walk.

Cairnkinna's cairn remains hidden from view until you come over the brow of the first small hill, and the route to the summit immediately becomes quite obvious. Around this time the terrain changes from green grass and bracken to boggier rough grassland, open and rolling. In some respects the landscape is similar to the broad flank of the Neive of the Spit (Walk 18, Merrick), but not as high, and in poor weather it could be very exposed up here.

It may look otherwise but the going is never very steep, although it can be quite rough underfoot in places. Continue on the broad flank of the hill round the corrie and follow the gradual incline uphill to the cairn. Standing about 4 metres high, it's a two tier dry-stone wall structure built on a covering of stones and very impressive, despite having fallen down a bit at the back.

It's worth spending a little bit of time at the summit admiring the fine view north-east to the Lowthers, south to Criffel and the sea and west to Benbrack and Cairnsmore of Carsphairn.

From the summit, head off down the broad east ridge towards the col between Mote Hill and Merkland Hill and a right-angled strip of forest to the right, following a fence. It's worth noting that some of the fences on this descent are electrified, although they all have safe modern gates or stiles and there's no area where you need come into contact with the wire.

As you descend towards the col there is a fine view down towards Woodend and the glen of the Scaur Water. Some of these lower fields have sheep in, so this section of the walk may not be possible at lambing time and you may have to descend to the right of the forest towards the Woodend Burn to join up with the track lower down.

Cross through the fields via some gates and fences until you arrive at a track in front of a wall. The track leads back easily to Woodend which can now be seen quite clearly in the distance. Before you get too low it's worth a final glimpse back, as the whole route round the cirque to the cairn is now revealed behind you.

Leaving the small wood at the start of the walk.

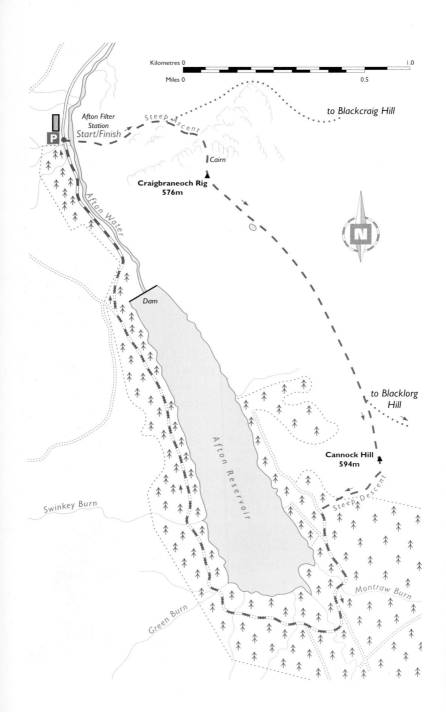

Kilometres 0   1.0

Miles 0   0.5

to Blackcraig Hill

Afton Filter Station
Start/Finish

Steep Ascent

Cairn

**Craigbraneoch Rig
576m**

Afton Water

N

Dam

*to Blacklorg
Hill*

Afton Reservoir

**Cannock Hill
594m**

Swinkey Burn

Steep Descent

Green Burn

Montraw Burn

FLOW GENTLY SWEET AFTON

This walk takes in the edge of the Carsphairn range of hills to the north of Cairnsmore of Carsphairn and Benbrack (Walk 5) and west of Cairnkinna (Walk 3).

East of Windy Standard, a cirque of hills form the head of Glen Afton, of which Alhang provides the source of the Afton Water which flows north to New Cumnock, where it swells the infant River Nith on its journey east and south to Dumfries and the Solway Firth.

This is a particularly fine glen which has provided recreation for people of Cumnock, Kilmarnock and Ayr for centuries. The Afton Water is described so lyrically by Robert Burns in his song Sweet Afton:

> Flow gently sweet Afton, among thy green braes,
> Flow gently, I'll sing thee a song in thy praise;
> My Mary's asleep by thy murmuring stream,
> Flow gently, sweet Afton, disturb not her dream.

Burns frequently stayed at New Cumnock while travelling between his farm at Ellisland north of Dumfries (see Walk 7) and Mossgiel just north of Mauchline where his mother, brother Gilbert and family lived. Burns lived at Mossgiel from 1784 to 1788, a significant period for the poet; his poetic genius burst into flower during those years and he met his wife Jean Armour. Mauchline, some 20 km north-west of New Cumnock, contains the imposing National Burns Memorial erected in 1896, and a small museum.

Legend has it that this song was written at the inn (the exact location of which scholars have been unable to determine) on the River Afton at New Cumnock. While travelling between Ellisland and Mossgiel, the poet stopped at the inn, then left to visit a Mr Logan of Laight, Glen Afton, for the evening.

During his absence news of the poet's presence spread quickly and a lively crowd gathered at the inn anticipating an entertaining evening. But, when Burns returned he appeared preoccupied with his thoughts

INFORMATION

Distance: 6½ km (4 miles)

Start and Finish: Public car-park, Afton Treatment Works. From New Cumnock follow the B741 Dalmellington road, turning left after a very short distance (signposted Caravan Site, Burns Cairn, Afton Treatment Works).

Terrain: Open hillside, forest track and road. Good boots are recommended. The section between Craigbraneoch Rig and Cannock Hill is cairned.

Map: OS Landranger, sheet 77, Dalmellington to New Galloway.

Refreshments: New Cumnock has full facilities.

and went straight to his room. In the morning he sent a servant to Laight with a draft of the song 'Clear Afton'.

The change of name is interesting as Burns appears to have titled it initially 'Clear Afton', later changing it to 'Sweet Afton'. A letter exists dated 5 February 1789 in which Burns encloses a copy of the song for Mrs Dunlop of Dunlop and states it is intended as a compliment to '. . . a small river, Afton near New Cumnock . . .'

Although much of the lower glen is probably little changed since Burns' day, forestry, a reservoir built in 1935 and a modern water treatment plant have changed the upper glen considerably. However, all the changes are fairly sympathetic with the landscape and they do ensure good access for walkers to enjoy the upper glen without considerable effort.

Retrace your path out of the public car-park and descend onto the road below which gives access to the reservoir. Just before the metal gate (which can also be accessed from the end of the public car-park) go left through a wooden gate and descend to the Afton Water. Cross the burn and climb the hillside ahead. Contour the hillside round and left, gaining height as you go, to pass below a small cliff. Continue round the hillside to a grassy ramp which then leads up and right and then left to the cairn on the summit of Craigbraneoch Rig.

The view down Glen Afton towards New Cumnock from the summit of Craigbraneoch Rig.

From here there are fine views north, straight down Glen Afton towards New Cumnock and the Ayrshire plain. To the north-east the bulk of Blackcraig Hill, at 700 m the highest hereabouts, dominates the view, looking especially impressive under snow or when misty. To the east is the lesser Blacklorg Hill and to the south the sweep of forest-fringed Afton Reservoir and behind Alwhat, Alhang, and in the distance, Windy Standard.

If you wanted to make a longer hillwalk it would be possible to continue contouring low below Craigbraneoch Rig, crossing the Craig Burn to ascend the west flank of Blackcraig Hill. From there you would walk south to Blackcraig Hill then west to Cannock Hill and north to descend over Craigbraneoch Rig. However, the route described here is less strenuous and designed to give a flavour of the area.

From the summit of Craigbraneoch Rig the next objective, Cannock Hill, can be seen quite clearly with a fence running up it. A good path, marked by cairns, leads to a corner of the fence with a gate. Go through the gate and ascend the hill, keeping right of the fence and the old wall.

At the top of Cannock Hill (594 m) the fence forms a corner before heading off east towards the flanks of Blacklorg Hill. It's worth taking in the fine views down to Afton reservoir and the hills around – and a short rest – as the descent from here to the reservoir requires care.

When you are ready leave the fence and continue in a southerly direction towards the small burn that runs along the edge of the forest. The hillside is steeper the further you go to the right directly overlooking the reservoir, so it is best to keep left. Follow the burn and the edge of the forest west and down towards the reservoir, taking care on a short section of grass and scree. Go through a short section of forest and you soon emerge onto the track round the reservoir.

With the energetic section of the walk over it's now possible to amble back round the reservoir in a clockwise direction, looking back to admire the hills you have traversed. At the reservoir drop down to the access road and walk back to the car-park.

On the way back down Glen Afton to New Cumnock it's worth stopping at the Burns Cairn erected by New Cumnock Burns Club on its golden jubilee, 1973. The cairn overlooks Afton Water on the right of the road and has laybys before and after.

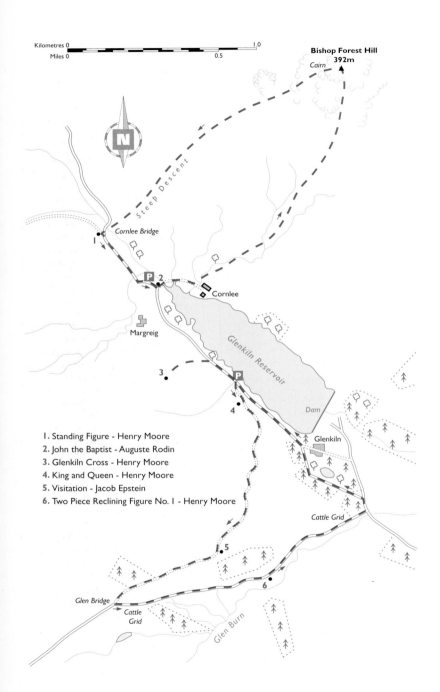

1. Standing Figure - Henry Moore
2. John the Baptist - Auguste Rodin
3. Glenkiln Cross - Henry Moore
4. King and Queen - Henry Moore
5. Visitation - Jacob Epstein
6. Two Piece Reclining Figure No. 1 - Henry Moore

THE GLENKILN SCULPTURES

There's nothing new about outdoor sculpture, especially when it comes to the work of Henry Moore, but good 'sculpture parks' are thin on the ground. Even then, most are specially set aside areas, parks or the grounds of a large house, where works are displayed in a semi-natural environment.

In this respect Glenkiln is a very special place. There's nothing unnatural about Glenkiln. It's a pleasant small glen, similar in many respects to many on the edge of Nithsdale and on the southern flanks of the Lowther Hills. Small rounded hills emerge from a pattern of green fields and white farmhouses, moorland and forestry.

However, the thing that makes Glenkiln unique in Britain, if not the world, is the imagination that has gone into siting six pieces of modern sculpture in a completely natural setting. The pieces by Henry Moore, Sir Jacob Epstein and Auguste Rodin are all quite close to the road and make an interesting centrepiece for a walk. The works were bought and placed by the landowner Sir William (Tony) Keswick, starting in 1951.

Two walks are described. The first over Bishop Forest Hill gives fine views over Glenkiln, while taking in two of the northernmost pieces of sculpture, and

INFORMATION

Distance: (a) Bishop Forest Hill, 5 km (3 miles); (b) Sculpture walk, 4 km (2½ miles).

Start and Finish: (a) The car-park near Cornlee farm; (b) The layby below the King and Queen. Glenkiln is reached by turning north off the A75 9 km west of Dumfries (signposted to Shawhead). At Shawhead turn right following signs for Dunscore then immediately left, still following signs for Dunscore, then left very soon after, signposted to Glenkiln. Follow the road down the glen alongside the reservoir, past Moore's King and Queen sculpture on the left and the Glenkiln Cross, high on to its right. At the end of the reservoir turn right and park.

Terrain: (a) Although this is a small hill, boots are recommended, as are waterproofs and a map and compass in poor weather; (b) Outdoor boots or shoes recommended.

Map: OS Landranger Sheet 84, Dumfries.

Winter light on the flanks of Bishop Forest Hill with Glenkiln Reservoir below.

provides pleasant hill-walking exercise. The second connects the remaining pieces and is easy walking on road and track. However, the remaining four pieces of sculpture can also be seen from the car.

Above the parking area is the John the Baptist sculpture by Rodin (1840–1917). The naked figure stands arm outstretched towards Glenkiln Reservoir, the light splashing on the body's features on a fine day.

From the car-park, walk up the track heading towards the pink washed buildings of Cornlee farm. At the end of the track, just before entering the farmyard there's a gate on the left. Go through this and up the side of a field and then out into rough ground to the north. Open ground leads up and left and on to Cornlee Hill, the broad south ridge of Bishop Forest Hill, which leads to the trig point on the summit. Despite the lowly height of 392 m, fine views can be had from the summit, with Dumfries and Criffel to the east and south and the hills of Nithsdale to the north.

Descend the west ridge towards the road and the bridge carrying it over the Shalloch Burn and Muil Burn. At the junction of the road and the track to Shalloch Farm is the Standing Figure by Henry Moore (1898–1986). Like much of Moore's work, it is a very abstract sculpture, so much so that when it arrived at Glenkiln, the gamekeeper, Mr Maxwell, took one look at it in its crate and thinking it must be a spare part for a tractor, sent it up to one of the farms!

Henry Moore's superb King and Queen sculpture overlooking Glenkiln Reservoir and Cornlee farm.

Unfortunately the sculpture was damaged in early 1995.

A short walk takes you back to the car and a short drive down the reservoir leads to a small layby below the Glenkiln Cross up on the hillside. The cross is the central part of a crucifixion triptych which can be seen in its entirety in London's Battersea Park as well as at Otterlo in Holland and Fort Worth, Texas. It can be visited by making a short walk uphill.

Further down the road is another small layby below Moore's King and Queen sculpture, which can be seen in the field on the right. The second walk starts from here and takes in this and two other pieces, unless of course the weather is poor or you have had enough walking. The King and Queen is one of Moore's more accessible pieces – they can be recognised as some actual human figure – and is considered to be among his finest works, serenely and rather amusingly gazing out over the reservoir.

If you continue up the hillside on the track that runs past the King and Queen you will arrive at Visitation by Sir Jacob Epstein (1880–1959). This figurative sculpture of the Virgin Mary looks down lower Glenkiln towards Shawhead, surrounded and complemented by a small circle of Scots pine. If you continue up this road, once used by Covenanters, perhaps on their way to meetings on the east side of Bishop Forest Hill, you will arrive at an old bridge beside a single track road.

John the Baptist showing the way above the car park at Cornlee farm.

Descend the road to the last piece of sculpture, Moore's Two Piece Reclining Figure No 1. The sculpture is Moore at his most abstract. It was lent to Tony Keswick by Moore and his daughter Mary Moore and was originally cast in bronze. However, after about 14 years Moore recalled the bronze, but replaced it with a fibreglass cast impregnated with bronze dust. The sculpture is placed on a 10-ton plinth selected from the local Mornington Quarry. Unfortunately its proximity to the road does mean that some graffiti has appeared, something thankfully absent from the other pieces.

To return to your car, descend the hill to a junction, turn left and follow the road alongside the reservoir.

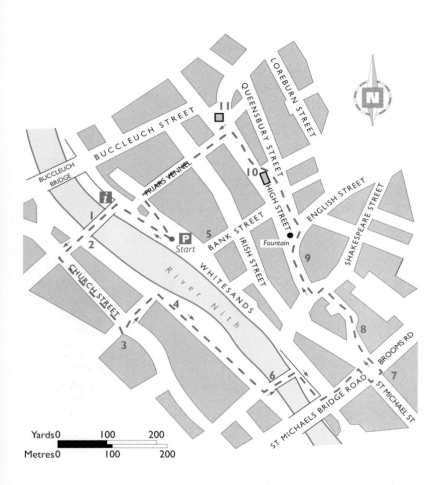

1. Devorgilla Bridge
2. Old Bridge House Museum
3. Dumfries Museum and Camera Obscura
4. Robert Burns Centre and Old Town Mill
5. Burns' House in Bank Street
6. Suspension Bridge
7. St Michael's Church and Burns Mausoleum
8. Burns' House in Burns Street (Mill Vennel)
9. Globe Inn
10. Mid Steeple
11. Burns' Statue

DUMFRIES

Dumfries stands at a point where the River Nith was both accessible to sea-going traffic from the Solway Firth and fordable by people and livestock. As such it is a classic river settlement and remains of occupation have been found which date back to the Stone Age (about 4000BC).

Guarded by the River Nith to the north and west and the now drained Lochar Moss to the east and south, the original settlement is thought to lie along the raised ridge of the High Street, linking the hills on which the present day St Michael's Church, Midsteeple and Greyfriars Church are built.

The earliest written reference is to Dronfries in 1150, possibly originating from the Celtic druim for a mound or ridge (or dun meaning a hillfort) and phreas meaning shrubs or brushwood. Dumfries grew during the 12th and 13th centuries as the Celts of Galloway were subdued and absorbed into a Scottish kingdom with help from strong Anglo-Norman families, many of whom later played a significant role in Scotland's monarchy; Bruce (founders of the Stuart line), Balliol and Comyn. During this time Dumfries became a royal burgh, protected by a royal castle, and grew rich on the trade between Scotland, Ireland and England.

Much of Dumfries' early history centres round the constant instability between England and Scotland, a running sore from the 13th to 16th centuries. Much of it has already been covered elsewhere in this book, so it is worth making a jump through two more centuries of religious and civil wars to the 18th century and a man who continues to attract interest from all over the world.

Robert Burns lived in the town from 1791 to his death in 1796. The walk described here visits a number of sites connected with Scotland's national bard and some places of local interest along the way.

INFORMATION

Distance: 2km (1¼ miles).

Start and Finish: Whitesands car-park

Terrain: Paths and pavements. No special footwear needed.

Map: A town guide is available at the tourist information centre and other shops.

Refreshments: Dumfries has full facilities.

Opening hours: *The Tourist Information* centre at Whitesands is open all year (call 01387 253862 for times). Toilets. Full details of the museums and attractions in this walk, opening times, costs etc can be obtained at the centre.

Other Activities: *Burns' farm* at Ellisland lies on the A76 about five miles north of Dumfries, GR 929838, and has a museum open to the public all year: 1000–1300; 1400–1700.

The walk starts at the tourist information centre at Whitesands, at one time a cattle market, beside the River Nith where there are a number of car parks.

Walk upstream towards the tourist information centre to cross the old bridge on the left. Known as the Devorgilla Bridge (see Walk 8, New Abbey), probably after an earlier wooden bridge, the present structure was built around 1430 by the Burgh of Dumfries and the Douglas family and partly rebuilt after flood damage in 1620. The three eastern arches were later removed, hence the rather sudden stepped approach. Buccleugh Street bridge to the north replaced it and was designed by local architect Thomas Boyd, who also designed and built Burns' farmhouse at Ellisland.

Devorgilla Bridge, Dumfries.

At the end of the Devorgilla Bridge is the Old Bridge House Museum with its stones to prevent carts clipping the sides. The building dates from 1660 and houses a collection of domestic articles from the 16th to 19th centuries. Ahead, a sign points up to Dumfries Museum. Follow the sign, turning left onto church street and then up to the museum and the white tower of the Camera Obscura.

The Camera Obscura started life as a windmill. This fell into disuse in 1834, but it was purchased and

Angling in the Nith at
Whitesands.

turned into an observatory the same year. The device
is still fully working and visitors can call in to watch
Dumfries at work and play for a small fee. The
museum was added later and in the grounds is a glass
rotunda enclosing a statue of Robert Paterson ('Old
Mortality') and his pony (see Walk 6, Caerlaverock

and Walk 19, Loch Trool) who died in 1801. The museum has a fascinating collection of items from different periods of history.

Follow the signs straight down the hill to the Robert Burns Centre on the riverside. From here there are fine views upstream to the old caul, or weir, and the Devorgilla Bridge. Across the Nith you can see the tower of the Midsteeple and Bank Street (called Wee Vennel, but better known as 'Stinking' Vennel in Burns' time), which descends from the High Street. On his arrival in Dumfries after leaving Ellisland, Burns lived in a flat on the first floor of number 11 where he produced some of his finest songs (see also Walk 10, Father of the American Navy).

Continue downstream and cross the 1875 suspension bridge. A right turn leads to St Michael's Bridge Road. Following the signs to Burns House and Mausoleum, turn left and climb a small hill to St Michael's Church on the right. To the south-east of the church is an indicator board showing the graves of Burns' friends, and at the back, the white dome of the Mausoleum. Interestingly, the Mausoleum was built in local red sandstone, but painted in the 1880s.

Burns' remains were moved to the Mausoleum in 1815 from his original grave in the cemetery. As seems to have happened frequently at this time, the actual building took a long time and was fraught with dispute between the mason, sculptor and the committee!

Return to the road and cross straight over to Burns' House, clearly signposted down on the right. On the crest of Burns Street, once called Mill Vennel, is the fine house which the Burns family moved to in 1793 and where Robert died three years later. The building is now a museum run by the district council. Descend Burns Street and turn into the pedestrianised High Street which has a new shopping centre on the left.

Walk up the High Street passing the close of the Globe Inn on the right, one of Burns' favourite inns, and then pass the fountain to rise up to the Midsteeple, built in 1707. It was here that Burns' body lay for three days in the court house before the impressive funeral procession to St Michael's Church.

Near the end of the High Street stood the old monastery of Grey Friars where Robert the Bruce murdered the Red Comyn, putting in motion the fight that would lead to Scotland's independence. The Burns Statue at the end of the High Street was designed by Amelia Hill and finally erected in 1882, although carved from Carrara marble by craftsmen in Italy.

From the statue turn left and descend the narrow Friars Vennel back to Whitesands.

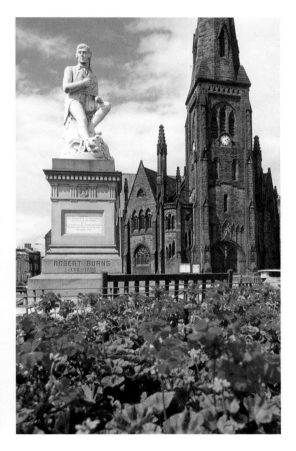

Burns' statue.

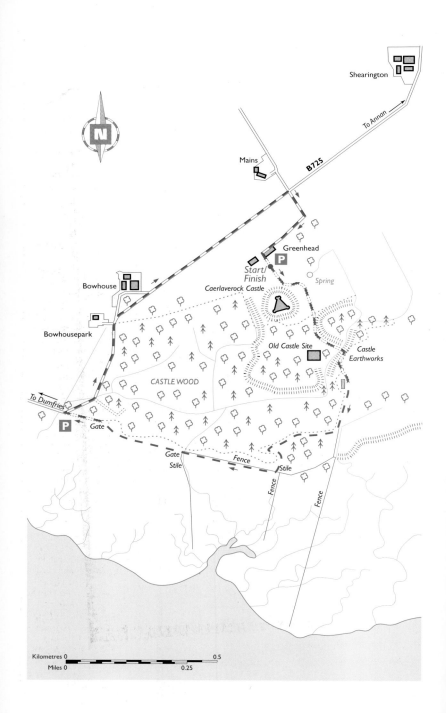

CAERLAVEROCK CASTLE AND NATURE RESERVE

I n some respects Caerlaverock Castle is rather out of place in Scotland, its 13th century solidity more akin to the border fortresses of Chepstow, Conwy or Caernarvon than Stirling, Edinburgh or the ornate baronial mansions and towers of the highlands and lowlands.

The castle was built in the late 13th century by the Maxwell family, wardens of the Western March, part of the boundary between Scotland and England. The heraldic panel over the main gate was erected by Robert Maxwell, 1st Earl of Nithsdale, in about 1634.

The impressive double tower of the gateway, extensive moat and high walls of red sandstone were built to resist attack and so they did, through countless sieges in the wars between Scotland and England. Robert the Bruce, Edward I and the Parliamentary forces during the English Civil War, all laid siege to the castle, the last-named dismantling the rear section of the building after a 13-week siege in 1640. The ruin eventually passed by descent into the hands of the Dukes of Norfolk and was given into the care of the state in 1946.

Caerlaverock's triangular shieldlike shape is unique among British castles and with its deep moat, extensive outer earthworks, landscaped grounds and children's play area it makes a perfect place for a family outing, followed by a walk to Caerlaverock National Nature Reserve on the coast. The castle is in the care of Historic Scotland and there is an entry charge, the only walk in this book that will actually cost you anything.

After touring the castle, the nature reserve is easily reached by following the road from the car-park that runs down beside the castle. It soon runs into woodland and then a clearing with a raised mound surrounded by a ditch is reached on the right. The

INFORMATION

Distance: 5 km (3 miles).

Start and Finish: Caerlaverock Castle. From Dumfries, take the B725 Bankend road south and follow it beside the Nith for 12 km to the castle car-park.

Terrain: Easy going, but wellingtons or boots are recommended for the nature reserve.

Map: OS Landranger Sheet 84, Dumfries

Refreshments: Caerlaverock Castle has toilets and a shop and there are toilets at the Wildfowl and Wetlands Trust site.

Opening Hours: *Caerlaverock Castle:* Apr–Sep. Mon–Sat 0930–1830, Sun 1400–1830. Oct–Mar, Mon–Sat 0930–1630, Sun 1400–1630. Admission charge. *Caerlaverock National Nature Reserve:* Entry is free and visitors are allowed to walk on the merse and mudflats. Please respect fences and any grazing livestock. *Wildfowl and Wetlands Trust, East Park:* The site lies about 4 km east of the castle and offers a number of modern hides where the birds of the merse can be observed. Weekend and holiday accommodation is also available. Open Oct-Apr, 10.00–17.00 daily. No dogs. Admission charge, WWT members free.

The impressive double tower and drawbridge of Caerlaverock Castle.

exact origins of this are unclear, but various suggestions have been made; a precursor to the existing castle, a supply depot linking the castle with the sea or a temporary structure used during a supposed period of dereliction of the main castle.

Continue on along the track through woodland and then open ground and pass some houses on the right.

The track turns into a path and enters fine woodland rich in holly, conifer, oak and silver birch. The path is a little overgrown in places, but it is well maintained with small bridges over the pools and small burns winding their way to the sea. Just before the coast is a fine area of open meadow with an abundance of grasses, wild flowers, thistles and butterflies in summer.

Pass through some final trees and cross a stile at a notice-board, to emerge on the merse of the Solway Firth with a fine view of the Lake District fells straight ahead, and Criffel and the Waterloo Monument to the right (see Walks 8 and 9).

On the Merse wetland of Caerlaverock National Nature Reserve, home of barnacle geese from Spitsbergen, Arctic Norway, with Criffel in the distance.

The nature reserve is of international importance as it provides the wintering grounds for the entire population of barnacle geese from Spitsbergen in Arctic Norway. Since its inception in 1957 the reserve has been a great success, seeing an increase in the numbers of barnacle geese from below 1000 in 1950 to almost 13,000.

Along with these geese, the reserve also plays home to pink-footed geese from Iceland and thousands of other wildfowl and waders including pintail, shelduck and oystercatchers. From October to February the geese roost on the sands and mudflats by night and feed on the merse or inland by day, and the best time to see them is when they leave their roosts at dawn.

The success of the barnacle geese on this 7710 hectare nature reserve is largely down to the decades of co-operation between governmental agencies (such as Scottish Natural Heritage, who manage the reserve), voluntary conservation bodies (such as the nearby Wildfowl and Wetlands Trust site at East Park), landowners, farmers and wildfowlers. However, because of their very numbers, the future of the barnacle geese is set to be a controversial issue.

Toadstool in the woods between the castle and nature reserve.

The next section of the walk can be quite muddy and wellingtons or other boots are probably a good idea. It's worth noting that the merse and mud flats can be dangerous in mist or south-westerly gales and during high tides. This walk together with other routes in and around the National Nature Reserve is illustrated in a recently published leaflet. To avoid the worst obstacles follow the numbered posts. The rare and protected natterjack toad also breeds on pools at the landward edge of the merse, which itself supports a distinct range of salt-tolerant plants such as thrift and sea aster.

Turn right and walk over the merse for about 15 minutes to a fence which can be crossed at a gate on the right or via a couple of stiles on the left. Continue to another gate on the right which is passed through and follow the track to a car-park. Turn right and follow the narrow country road round some bends and then uphill. A right-hand bend then leads to a straight, along which Caerlaverock Castle can be seen poking its head up on the right. Turn right and follow the short road through the arched gateway and back to the castle.

On your return to Dumfries it is worth making a quick visit to the parish church about half a mile north of Bankend (GR 026 692) where Robert Paterson is buried. Paterson was the basis of 'Old Mortality' in the book of the same name by Sir Walter Scott (see Glen Trool and Dumfries walks). The minister of the church Rev William McMorine baptised Robert Burns' daughter Elizabeth Riddell Burns in 1792 and officiated at the poet's funeral in 1776 (see also Walk 6, Dumfries).

The track linking Caerlaverock Castle and the National Nature Reserve.

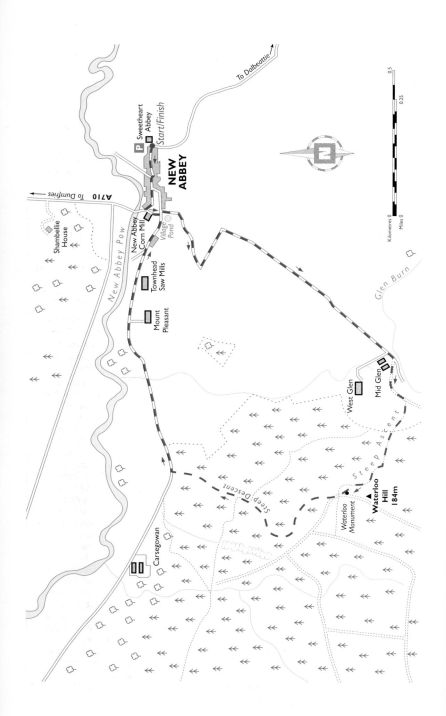

NEW ABBEY AND THE WATERLOO MONUMENT

Founded in 1273, Sweetheart Abbey is the best preserved of the three Cistercian abbeys in Galloway. It is also the youngest, hence the name New Abbey; 'new' in relation to the mother-house of Dundrennan, founded in about 1142.

The name Sweetheart comes from the founder Devorgilla de Balliol (see also Walk 6, Dumfries and Walk 19, Loch-Trool). A rich and influential woman, and a member of the Scots Royal Family, she was devoted to her husband John Balliol. On his death in 1269, she had his heart embalmed and placed in a silver-enamelled ivory casket which she carried everywhere. On her death in 1290 aged 80, she and the casket were buried together in the church of the abbey she had founded. It was the Cistercian monks who took the name Sweetheart, or Dulce Cor, for the abbey.

Sweetheart Abbey and the heirs of Devorgilla continue to figure in the following 50 years of Anglo-Scottish warfare. Her son John Balliol was appointed by Edward I of England in preference to the older Robert Bruce and reigned for four years, and her son-in-law John 'Red' Comyn was murdered by Robert the Bruce in Dumfries in 1306. The Scots crown returned to the Balliols when her son Edward was crowned in 1332. The first abbot John paid allegiance to Edward I and later, when Edward invaded Galloway, he stayed at Sweetheart.

By the Reformation in 1560, the abbey was staffed by an abbot and 15 monks. The last abbot, Gilbert Broun, retired to France in 1587, but returned to Scotland in 1589, continuing to hold publicly to the old faith.

Arrested at Sweetheart in 1603, he was imprisoned at Blackness Castle near Linlithgow before being allowed back to France. By 1608 he was back in Sweetheart.

INFORMATION

Distance: 4 km (2½ miles).

Start and Finish: Sweetheart Abbey car park, New Abbey. From Dumfries take the A710 coast road south for 10 km to New Abbey village and follow signs to the car park

Terrain: Roads and good tracks, although some could be a little muddy in places. Worth taking binoculars. The route to the monument is waymarked.

Map: OS Landranger Sheet 84, Dumfries.

Refreshments: Shops, cafes, pubs and post office in New Abbey.

Opening Hours: *Sweetheart Abbey:* Apr-Sep, Mon-Sat 0930–1830, Sun 1400–1830; Oct-Mar, Sat-Wed 0930–1630, Thurs 0930–1200, Sun 1400–1630. Admission charge. *New Abbey Corn Mill:* same opening times as the Abbey. Admission charge. You can get a joint ticket to both places at a reduced charge. *Shambellie House Museum of Costume* is about 10 minutes walk north of New Abbey. The collection of Victorian costume is part of the National Museums of Scotland. Open Apr-Oct. 1100–1700. Admission charge.

The pond at New Abbey at the start of the road leading to the Waterloo Monument.

The following year, on the authority of the Archbishop of Glasgow, his room was broken into and 'a great number of Popish books, copes, chalices, pictures, images and other such Popish trash' were removed. All save the books were publically burned one market day in Dumfries' High Street. The abbot seems to have retired to Paris and died there in 1612.

Sweetheart was saved from demolition by the Maxwell family, but later sold for the stone. Roofless by 1779, it was purchased from the owners by a local consortium, but most of the outer buildings were removed, leaving only the gateway into the cloisters remaining. It passed into state care in 1928.

Having viewed the abbey, walk down the main street of New Abbey. At the end down on the right just before the bridge is the historic New Abbey Corn Mill, which is open to the public and is well worth a visit. Further up the road on the left is Shambellie House Museum of Costume, part of the National Museums of Scotland.

The first turning on the left, just before the corn mill, leads to the village duck pond. With benches and grass it's a pleasant place for a picnic. Just before the pond, a signpost on the left directs you north along the road which leads to the Waterloo Monument. The road follows the pond then rises quite steeply to swing sharp left, with views down onto the village and Sweetheart Abbey, and then right. The monument can be seen up on the right with Criffel rising to the left.

The road ends at a white building on the right and a wooden bridge over a small burn. Another signpost 'To the Waterloo Monument' points to a path into trees on the right. Cross a stile and follow the path through a small section of wood and then over a track. Another stile leads into a conifer forest and a very steep path, expertly made from stones embedded into the slope.

Come out of the forest and the tower is straight ahead. A stone spiral staircase leads to the top from where there are panoramic views of Criffel, Shambellie House, Dumfries and New Abbey, and Caerlaverock. The tower is about 20 m high and completely open at the top, so children should be accompanied by an adult.

The view from below the Waterloo Monument over Loch Kindar, with the Solway Firth in the distance.

The monument was erected in 1816, 'To record the valour of those British, Belgian and Prussian soldiers who under Wellington and Blucher on the 18th of June 1815 gained the victory of Waterloo by which French tyranny was overthrown and peace restored to the world', and is typical of many put up at that time.

From here it is possible to return the same way, but a round route can be had by descending in the opposite direction. The path starts with a few slippery roots and it's worth being a little careful. A path, muddy in places, leads down through conifer forest. Go left on a forest track, and follow the track downhill for a few yards until a sign indicates right onto another path back into the forest. There has been a reasonable amount of tree felling going on around here, so the landscape may change in the future. The signposts are marked with green and white arrows and a little symbol of a tower in white.

Descend with a burn on your left (a bit of bushwhacking may be needed to clear bracken in the late summer), to new conifer plantations, clearings and an area of mature broadleaf woodland. The path comes out onto a track with a signpost pointing back up the hill to the Waterloo Tower.

Follow this very pleasant track with the tower up on the hillside on the right, until it turns into a road which leads back to the duck pond in New Abbey.

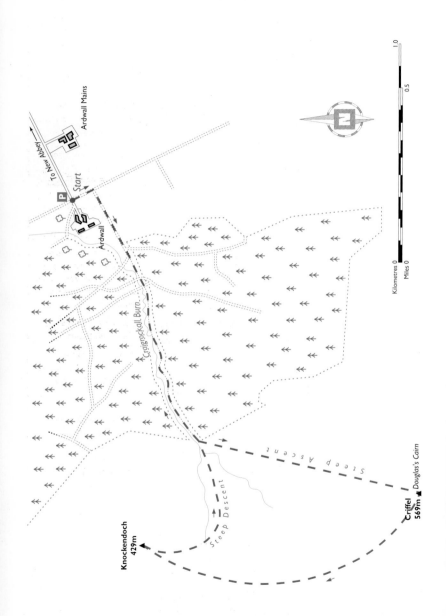

CRIFFEL

*'The Nith shall run to Corsincon,
And Criffel sink in Solway,
Ere we permit a foreign foe
On British ground to rally!'*

So wrote Robert Burns in *Does Haughty Gaul Invasion Threat*, written in 1795 among rumours of imminent invasion by Napoleon.

The fine little mountain of Criffel overlooks the sands and mudbanks of the estuary of the River Nith and, when viewed from the high ground to the east of Dumfries, provides a splendid backdrop to the town.

The origins of the name are unclear; it is possibly from the Scandinavian kraka fjall or the lowland Scottish craw fell – both meaning raven's or crow's hill. Whatever the origins, it's a fine vantage point and a good introduction to hillwalking; high enough for the going to become quite rough in places, but not so high that it is serious. However, as with all mountain walks it should not be underestimated; bad weather is attracted to 'huge Criffel's hoary top', as William Wordsworth put it, and the summit path is indistinct in places.

From the parking place, a large gate on the left capped with barbed wire gives access to a track and after a few hundred metres, a signpost on the right gives directions to Criffel.

INFORMATION

Distance: 6 km (4 miles).

Start and Finish: Ardwall farm. From Dumfries take the A710 coast road south for 15 km through New Abbey and turn right to Ardwall. There is limited parking. Please comply with the signs requesting drivers to leave clear access for farm machinery at all times.

Terrain: Boots are recommended as are waterproofs and a map and compass in poor weather.

Map: OS Landranger sheet 84, Dumfries.

Refreshments: Shops, cafes, pubs and post office in New Abbey.

Other Activities: *New Abbey* close by has a number of attractions (see walk 8).

The ruins of Sweetheart Abbey with Criffel behind.

Looking down the flanks of Criffel towards the Craigrockhall Burn through the forest. New Abbey and Dumfries beyond.

This track, lined with bluebells and butterflies in the spring, then leads slightly uphill past the farm with the tower of the Waterloo Monument (see Walk 8) rising above the farm and Loch Kindar on the right. The loch contains a crannog, a manmade island of stones which once held a round house. Most of the crannogs in south-west Scotland, and there are a lot of them as a look at the Dumfries OS map sheet will show, date from the end of the 1st millenium BC to the 1st century AD.

At the track end is a gate and a path continuing into a forest. After a short distance the Craigrockall Burn is reached and a forestry road crossed. Follow the burn through pleasant forest scenery. The going is a little boggy in places, but nothing that can't be avoided, and you emerge out of the forest and onto the open moorland after about half an hour. On the left, the signposted path rises to the summit of Criffel and on the right is the subsidiary summit of Knockendoch.

It's worth stopping at this point and taking in the view down the ride through the forest to the pattened green and brown fields with their white farmhouses and on to the mudflats and the estuary of the River Nith. The path to the summit becomes quite rough and boggy in places before leveling out after about half an hour onto

Loch Kindar and its crannog, the small round island, from Criffel. Caerlaverock and the River Nith mudflats in the distance.

the rounded summit plateau. Carry on to a pile of stones marking the large summit cairn, known as Douglas' Cairn, and trig point.

The views are extremely fine, especially across the Solway to the hills of the Lake District. From the summit the path cuts off to the left to follow the shoulder linking Criffel and Knockendoch. This well marked path takes a line just down from the crest of the shoulder, overlooking the path up from the farm. Once again the going can be quite boggy in places but not too bad.

From the shoulder Knockendoch looks quite impressive and rather steep, but this is deceptive and the summit is no distance at all. This is a very pleasant summit marked with a small cairn and has more interesting and more open views than Criffel itself. Over to the left, Sweetheart Abbey and the Waterloo Monument can be seen quite clearly.

The northerly ridge of Knockendoch can be descended all the way to New Abbey, but this would involve a long walk back along the A710 to the car at Ardwall, so it is best to descend via the ascent route. From the summit descend in a south-easterly direction to pick up the approach path where it emerges from the forest and reverse your steps alongside the Craigrockall Burn to the car.

NOTE: There is an unfortunate tendency for people to leave litter at the summit of Criffel. If you come across any please try to pick it up and avoid leaving any yourself.

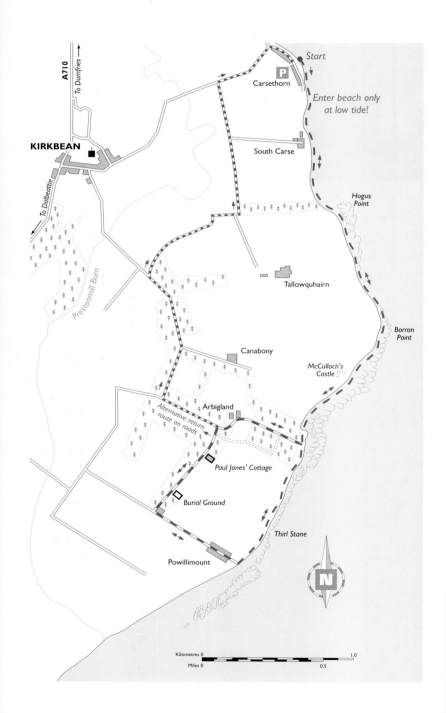

A710

To Dumfries →

KIRKBEAN

To Dalbeattie

Prestonmill Burn

Carsethorn

Start

Enter beach only
at low tide!

South Carse

Hogus
Point

Tallowquhairn

Borron
Point

Canabony

McCulloch's
Castle

Arbigland

Alternative return
route on roads

Paul Jones' Cottage

Burial Ground

Thirl Stane

Powillimount

N

Kilometres 0 _____ 1.0
Miles 0 _____ 0.5

FATHER OF THE AMERICAN NAVY

A hero to the Americans, a traitor to the British; the name of John Paul Jones has evoked different responses from historians through the centuries since his death in Paris in 1792. What has never been in doubt was the supreme seamanship of the man born the son of a gardener at Arbigland House, and credited by many as 'Father of the American Navy'.

This walk to Jones' birthplace follows a section of coastline that would have been familiar to the naval adventurer.

Born John Paul in 1747, he went to sea at the age of 12, alternating between periods living in Scotland and sailing from Whitehaven and London to the West Indies. By 1773 he was resident in Virginia, America, having added the name 'Jones' to his own, some historians say after an incident in which the leader of a mutiny was killed. Whatever the reason he was commissioned into the American continental navy in 1775, spending the next two years harassing the British navy in the West Indies.

By 1778 he was based in France from where he was engaged in a number of actions, attacking Whitehaven on the morning of 23rd April 1778 and then Kirkcudbright later that day with the intention of capturing the Earl of Selkirk. The Earl was not present, but some silver plate was seized. The articles were later returned to Lady Selkirk in 1785 at the insistence of Benjamin Franklin (it is said they still had tea leaves in the tea pots).

In September, accompanied by two other ships, he made a daring raid up the Firth of Forth, getting to within gunshot of Leith before a fierce squall forced them back into the firth. Deciding to make the best of their presence they attacked a British merchant convoy returning from the Baltic and captured the leading escort, the *Serapis*, although at the loss of Jones' own ship.

INFORMATION

Distance: 11 km (7 miles).

Start and Finish: Carsethorn car-park. From Dumfries take the A710 coast road through New Abbey and Kirkbean to Carsethorn.

Terrain: Roads and beach. The beach can be quite rough and stout shoes are recommended. It should be noted that the stretch of coast round Barron Point can be impassable at high tide.

Map: OS 1:50,000 sheet 84, Dumfries.

Refreshments: Carsethorn has a pub, shop, telephone and toilets.

Opening hours: *The John Paul Jones Cottage and Museum:* Apr.-Sept., Tues.-Sun. 1000–1700; July-Aug., 1000–1700, all week. Admission charge. *Arbigland House Gardens:* May-Sept., Tues.-Sun., 1400-1800; check for Bank Holiday opening. Admission charge.

Jones put into Texel in Holland in the Serapis, but the Dutch refused to recognise the American flag and he had to break out in one of the smaller ships and head back to France. He returned to Philadelphia in 1781, but did not command another American ship, sailing instead with the French and then in 1788 with the Russians for a year as a rear-admiral. He returned to Paris where he died in 1792. His unmarked grave lay undiscovered until 1905 when his supposed remains were returned to America with a US Navy escort and laid to rest in the chapel of the Naval Academy in Annapolis, Maryland.

Travelling through Kirkbean it is worth stopping for a moment at the parish kirk, which has a strong connection with Robert Burns who was a frequent visitor to the coast while working for the excise (see Walks 6 and 13), and contains a font presented by the Americans in memory of John Paul Jones.

From the large car park beside the beach at Carsethorn, start walking south along the pleasant sandy beach with views back to Criffel and across the Solway back to Caerlaverock and the Lake District. The route continues along the beach, sometimes on sand or shells, with some rockier ground to traverse Hogus Point. Care should be taken on the sandstone which can be quite slippery and give rough going. Continue round Borron Point, and follow the high water mark above the rocky coastline. Great care should be taken as this stretch can be impassable at high tide.

After a short distance you go past a building and then there is a small sea wall on the right with a set of steps leading to a black gate with sign indicating private grounds; this is the foot of Arbigland House garden. The path continues at high water level round the beach and then rises above the beach to follow a wall through a wood, before descending to the splendid Thirlstane rock, bored through by the action of the sea. Follow the sandy beach to the car-park at Powillimount.

The Thirlstane, an eroded sandstone cliff on the shore near Powillimount.

Looking south the lighthouse at Southerness can be seen quite clearly. The name probably comes from the Scandinavian saltr nes – salt point – as salt pans were worked here as far back as the 13th century. The square rubble-built lighthouse, one of the earliest in Scotland, was built in 1748 by Oswald of Auchencruvie, to guide ships, and no doubt smugglers and pirates, up the Solway.

Turn right at the car-park, Arbigland Estate Trustees sign, and follow the track through the farmyard to the road; the top of Arbigland House and the white John Paul Jones cottage can be seen on the right. Turn right at the first building with a gate in the wall ('private' sign designed to deter excessive car use), and pass a small cemetery to arrive at a large car-park beside John Paul Jones' cottage where there is a small museum depicting Jones' life and times.

The Cross of St Andrew and the Stars and Stripes flying outside John Paul Jones' cottage.

Three choices are now possible. You can visit Arbigland House gardens (admission charge), and exit from the gate at the bottom, returning along the beach, or return along the road with or without visiting the gardens. To return via the road, turn left up the drive opposite the gateway to the house and then right down the hill towards Criffel. Take the first turning right, signposted Nethermill and Talquerhain, to another T-junction. The road on the right, marked no through road, leads back to Carsethorn. The distance from Arbigland to Carsethorn is about 3 km along open country lanes.

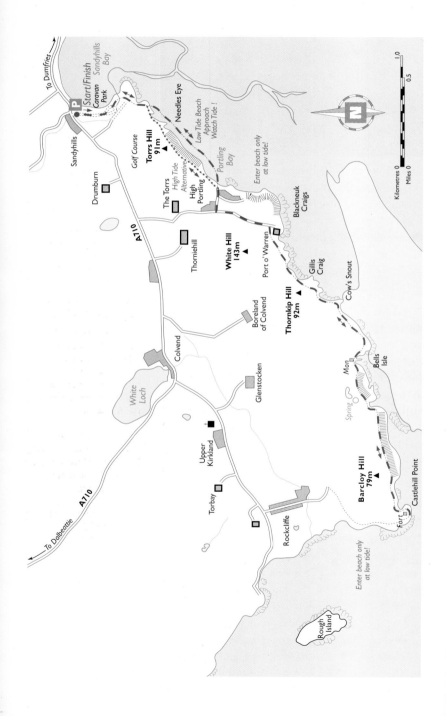

SANDYHILLS TO ROCKCLIFFE

The magnificent sandy beach and impressive cliffs at Sandyhills Bay give some of the finest coastal walking on the Solway coast. At about 12 km round trip this is quite a long walk, but it has the convenience of being able to be broken at Portling, a round walk of only 5 km.

Before going to Sandyhills it's worth finding out the state of the tides (most of the national newspapers publish the times of high tides at ports around the UK). Having some idea of the tide is useful as the first section from Sandyhills Bay to Portling can be walked along the shore or inland, and it gives some variety to be able to walk one way out and a different way back.

From the car-park, head around to the right to a wooden bridge which crosses the deep channel flowing into the bay. After crossing the bridge continue straight on to a signpost. From here you can go right, over the hill, or left, down onto the beach and walk along the shore. If you decide to take the cliff top path then go right and up some banks, covered in bluebells in the summer. The path climbs to the summit of Torr Hill and an indicator board gives you a chance to admire the extensive views to the Lake District and the sandflats. Then descend to Portling.

If you take the shore option, then be warned that the tide comes in quickly and it would be possible to get trapped between the water and the cliffs in a number of places.

About 10 minutes along the beach you arrive at a spectacular arch of rock. All the way along here the cliffs of red sedimentary rock are covered with a bright yellow lichen. The small hamlet of Portling with its painted houses, jetty and lifebelt is reached in a further 10 minutes.

At this point it is possible to scramble along the shore over seaweed covered boulders to Port o'Warren, but it is much easier to head inland. Gain the road and walk

---

INFORMATION

Distance: 12 km (7½ miles).

Start and Finish: Sandyhills Bay car-park (there is a charge for parking at some periods of the year). From Dumfries take the A710 coast road for 27 km through New Abbey and Kirkbean to Sandyhills.

Terrain: Sandy sea-shore and good cliff paths. Most of the route is well signposted.

Map: OS Landranger sheet 84, Dumfries.

Refreshments: *Tourist Information Centre* (seasonal) and toilets at Sandyhills Bay, plus shops and hotels. Hotel and cafe in Rockcliffe.

Other Activities: Access to the National Trust Bird Sanctuary at Rough Island is open to the public at certain times of the year. Check with NTS for times and dates.

The impressive arch of the Needle's Eye on the Mersehead Sands beyond Sandyhills Bay.

up the hill to a junction with a signpost. Turn left and follow the tarmaced road uphill and then go down the track on the other side. Near the bottom of the track a signpost on the right indicates the continuation of the path to Rockcliffe.

Follow the path up the hillside through gorse bushes, giving a heady sweet scent in the spring, until the top of the cliff overlooking Port o'Warren is reached. Keeping on the cliff top, cross gorse-covered fields via stiles to an impressive view back to the Cow's Snout, the large guano-covered cliff which plunges into the water beyond Port o'Warren and is often busy with swirling guillemots and cormorants. Beyond the cliff you can pick out Southerness lighthouse and across

The steep crags of the Cow's Snout beyond Port o'Warren.

the Solway Firth, the ever-present fells of the Lake District.

Continue down alongside walls and over stiles, until on the left above some small cliffs and very close to the sea is a memorial shaped like the top of a rocket (marked 'Mon' on the OS map). A plaque on the monument reads: 'The schooner Elbe, Captain Samuel Wilson of Palnackie, after providentially landing her crew here, backed off the rocks and sank off Rascarrel – 6th Dec 1866.' (See also Walk 13, Balcary Point).

The sound of waves crashing is never far away as you walk above the sandy inlets of this section of the coast, and even on a sunny day it isn't difficult to imagine the devastation the rocks could do to a wooden-hulled ship in a winter storm.

Barcloy Hill is skirted on its left-hand side, following a footpath close to the wall which is signposted and has an arrow painted on a rock. After climbing up the hill a bit, the wall continues up to the right and the path splits off left, continuing round the hillside on a well worn and obvious path.

Down below is the impressive Castlehill Point jutting out into the sea with the

In spring the smell of the gorse on the cliff tops is overwhelming.

remains of a hill fort on top. Barcloy fort is thought to date from about late Stone Age, or early Iron Age (about 1000BC to 500BC), one of many scattered in commanding positions around this coast (see also Walk 12, Balcary Point). The plaque at the fort places it at 4000BC in the Stone Age which seems too early for such a fortified settlement.

A section of wall 3 m thick can be seen and the fort is guarded from the mainland by a broad rock-cut ditch with a rampart on the outer lip. Early mediaeval pottery found inside can now be seen in Dumfries Museum.

An indicator board on the top of the hill points to surrounding landmarks along the Solway coast. Having admired the scenery it is possible to descend into Rockcliffe village before returning via the same route to Sandyhills Bay, with the same option of beach or cliff top, depending on the state of the tide.

If the tide is low on your arrival and you are outside the nesting season, then it is possible to walk the causeway over to Rough Island off Rockcliffe. The island is owned and managed by the National Trust for Scotland as a bird sanctuary.

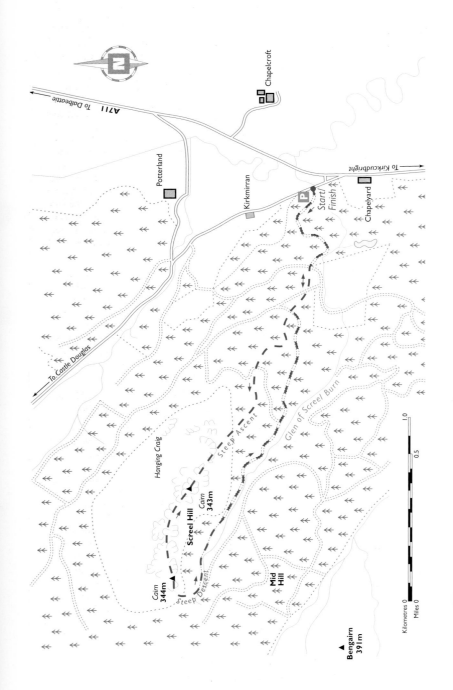

To Dalbeattie
A711
Chapelcroft
Potterland
Kirkmirran
To Kirkcudbright
Start/Finish
P
Chapelyard
To Castle Douglas
Hanging Craig
Steep Ascent
Glen of Screel Burn
Screel Hill
Cairn 343m
Cairn 344m
Steep Descent
Mid Hill
Bengairn 391m

Kilometres 0   0.5   1.0
Miles 0

SCREEL HILL

Height alone should never be the sole criterion in deciding whether a hill is worth the effort of ascent. Some of the largest hills in Scotland are uninteresting lumps with poor views, while other lowly hills have a view totally out of proportion to their size. Screel Hill falls into this latter category. On a scale of 1 to 10 the view from the top on a good day is 9.99! The hill is also a good example of interesting forest walking.

In some ways the coastal location is similar to Criffel. Screel pokes its bare rocky head from a skirt of dark forest and green fields dotted with white and pink farmhouses. To the east, fields lead gently down to the islands and craggy promontories of Auchencairn Bay and the mouth of the Urr Water.

From the car-park, a gate on the left gives access to a track waymarked with green posts with a white band. The track rises up through the forest, continuously rising and twisting but never very steep.

After a short distance you come out into the open at a track junction. The path is marked by a post and a green rail straight ahead and leads back into the forest. In the autumn the ground at the base of the trees hereabouts is thick with *Amanita muscarina* and other toadstools and if you are carrying an identification book, it will be much thumbed by the end of the walk.

The path now enters an area of much denser and newer woodland with a thick carpet of brown needles. This is a dark and quite spooky section of the walk – it's easy to see where the ancient tales of forest spirits came from. The marker posts continue, although some are missing in places and you have to keep a close watch as the posts are easily hidden in the gloom.

Come out of the gloomy bit of forest and cross a track. It is worth taking a look around at this point as the track taken on the return comes in from the left to rejoin the path. A more open and brighter area of

INFORMATION

Distance: 5½ km (3½ miles).

Start and Finish: Screel Hill car-park. From Dumfries, take A711 south-west through Dalbeattie. About 8 km south of Dalbeattie, past the turning to Potterland farm, there is a large car-park on the right signposted 'Forestry Commission Screel Wood, Screel Hill Walk'.

Terrain: Forest tracks and hill paths, stout footwear is recommended. The route has regular waymarks. On a good day a pair of binoculars will add considerable interest.

Map: OS 1:50,000, Sheet 84, Dumfries.

Refreshments: None en route. Nearest in Dalbeattie.

Other Activities: The nearby *Doach Wood* has two walks along forest tracks. Although the walking is pleasant the views are less interesting. The wood was planted in 1925 and is of particular interest for its 40 m Douglas Fir trees.

younger trees now follows with a more obvious path. After a while you arrive at a small clearing and there's a bench on the left with a pleasant enough view, but only a small taste of what is to come.

A small section of forest follows – the path can be a bit muddy underfoot – and then you are out onto open hillside. The waymarks continue and the pleasant rocky path is very obvious, rising uphill to the left of some crags. On a sunny autumn day the contrast between the brown and bright green of the bracken and the brown and purple of the heather is fantastic.

Ascend the path for a short distance towards Bengairn, the higher hill over to the left with a trig point on top,

and then turn round and admire the view. Over to the left in the far distance is the coast at Caerlaverock, then Criffel, Southerness lighthouse and Sandyhills Bay. Closer to, Rockcliffe and Castlehill Point and Barcloy Hill (see Walk 11), Rough Island, Hestan Island and on the right Balcary Point (see Walk 13). In the foreground among the fields is Orchardton House and further to the left the top of Orchardton Tower may even be seen.

The view from the flanks of Screel Hill across Auchencairn Bay to the Solway Firth. On the left are Barcloy Hill and Castlehill Point (Walk 11) and on the right Almorness Point and Hestan Island.

A steep little section of path brings you up onto the top of the first hill from where the best views are possible. Follow the well worn path north-west away from the coast across the broad, rather marshy shoulder separating the first top from the main summit. The view from the higher summit is interesting, but not nearly as grand. Bengairn has a prominent position on the left with the broad top of Cairnsmore of Fleet in the distance. Closer are the houses of Castle Douglas fronted by Carlingwark Loch, and further to the left you may be able to see the superb ruins of Threave Castle on an island in the River Dee. The castle is well worth a visit. Further to the right Dalbeattie comes into view and then acres of forestry plantation to Criffel's broad summit and the coast.

It is possible to return the way you came, but there is also a very pleasant return route back through the forest. From the top of Screel Hill head towards Bengairn and pick up the waymarks again, heading downhill on an obvious path to the col between Screel Hill and Mid Hill.

Orchardton Tower – a unique round-tower in Scotland.

Follow a wall, wet underfoot in places, then turn left into the forest and start to descend. After a short while you enter an impressive arched tunnel of tree branches through the forest. Underfoot, a carpet of brown needles makes for very pleasant walking, but keep an eye out for exposed tree roots which can be extremely slippery even in dry weather.

The tunnel eventually ends at a more conventional forest track which leads back to where the ascent path crossed the track. Turn right and enter the dark forest, taking care to follow the waymarks, which are even less clear in descent. Retrace your steps to the car-park.

After the walk it is worth driving a short distance to view Orchardton Tower, signposted from the A711 about 1.5 km north of the turning to the Screel Hill car-park. This 20 m tower-house was built towards the end of the 15th century for John Cairns, laird of Orchardton. The building is unique because it is the only existing cylindrical tower-house in Scotland. No others are recorded as having been built, most tower-houses of this date like MacLellan's Castle, visited on Walk 13, being rectangular.

The balustrade on the walkway at the top of Orchardton Tower.

The tower is open to the sky, but a number of rooms can be explored and there is a stone spiral stairway leading to a roof-top balustrade which gives fine views of Screel Hill and the surrounding countryside. The outer ruins are the remains of contemporaneous adjoining buildings.

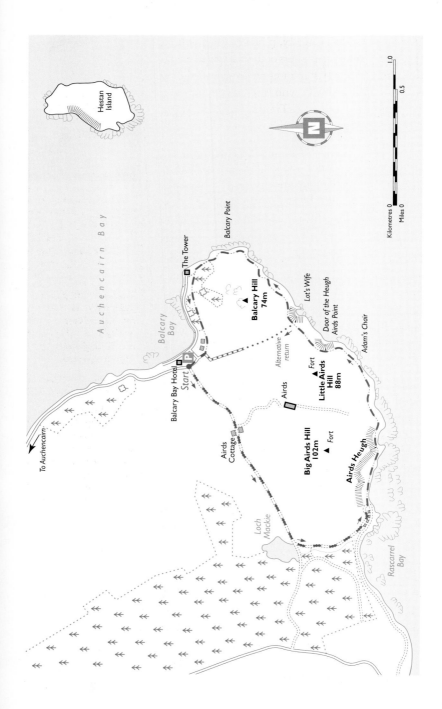

Hestan Island

Auchencairn Bay

To Auchencairn

Balcary Bay

The Tower

Balcary Point

Balcary Bay Hotel

Start

P

Balcary Hill
74m

Lot's Wife

Door of the Heugh

Airds Point

Alternative return

Adam's Chair

Airds

Little Airds
Hill
88m

Fort

Airds
Cottage

Big Airds Hill
102m

Fort

Airds Heugh

Loch Mackie

Rascarrel Bay

Kilometres 0
Miles 0

0.5

1.0

N

BALCARY POINT

In the late 16th century, piracy was a common occurrence and the waters of the Irish Sea were no exception. Scottish pirates prospered, including one Leonard Robertson who is recorded as having seized the Chester-bound *Trinity of Helberie* in the River Dee and then returned home to Kirkcudbright and sold the cargo.

Little seems to have been done about the incident; Queen Elizabeth I complained to King James and a local committee was set up to investigate. Nothing came of this, however, as some members of the committee had bought the cargo!

The real battle between customs and excise and the smugglers did not begin in earnest until the 1707 union of Scotland and England. The tidal creeks and bays of the rocky Solway coast were perfect for smuggling; the safe anchorage at Balcary Bay was notorious and reports exist of salt, tea, spirits and tobacco all being smuggled ashore from the bay.

The main section of what is now the Balcary Bay Hotel was built in the 18th century by the Manx company Clark, Grain and Quirk and contains a vault in the basement for storing contraband. Most of these goods came from the Isle of Man which had very low duty on many products and small boats made the easy journey across the Solway.

One well-known story tells of a young Manxman in the 1780s, eager to make money for his wedding. Running a cargo into the mouth of the Urr Water in an open boat he was surprised by an excise cutter from Balcary Bay (possibly the King's Boat from Carsethorn near Kirkbean). Failing to heave-to when ordered, he was fired upon and killed. His fiancée and members of both families later came over from the Isle of Man for his body, but as they left the mouth of the Urr beside Hestan Island a sudden squall came up, the boat overturned and all were drowned.

INFORMATION

Distance: 5 km (3 miles).

Start and Finish: at the car-park outside Balcary Bay Hotel. From Dumfries take A711 through Dalbeattie and continue to Auchencairn. A signposted no through road going left at the north end of Auchencairn leads in 3 km to the Balcary Bay Hotel and a large car-park.

Terrain: Mostly good paths and tracks, but they can be very muddy where they pass through fields. Regular signposts.

Map: OS Landranger sheet 84, Dumfries.

Refreshments: The Balcary Bay Hotel is open to non-residents and has full facilities, otherwise the nearest shops are at Auchencairn.

A fictionalised version of Hestan Island is at the centre of S. R. Crockett's smuggling novel *The Raiders* (see also Walk 18, Merrick). A frequent visitor to the town and villages of the coast from 1788 to 1795 was Scotland's bard and excise officer Robert Burns. By the middle of the 19th century the arrival of more revenue cutters, coastguard boats and the navy led to a reduction in smuggling, although it continued until the 1920s.

This walk starts from outside the Balcary Bay Hotel and takes in Rascarrel Bay, another haunt of smugglers and some impressive sea cliff scenery.

Near the hotel entrance follow a signposted track up through open green fields overlooked by Screel Hill and Bengairn (see Walk 12), towards Rascarrel Bay. At a junction go straight ahead, signposted to Loch Mackie and Rascarrel, past a white farmhouse with curling stones on the gateposts. A gate leads past an abandoned cottage on the right and then to another gate and a field, frequently filled with cows. The field track is good, but can be very muddy.

In no time at all you start to descend to the reed fringed edge of Loch Mackie, with its 'Private Fishing' sign hovering Excalibur-like in the centre. If the wind is in the right direction you should be able to hear the waves breaking at Rascarrel Bay to the south. Cross the stile and walk in the direction of the sign pointing to the shore. Up on the left is Big Airds Hill with its trig point and hill fort.

Continue on the track towards the shore – the going can be muddy underfoot – and emerge at Rascarrel's

Looking across Auchencairn Bay towards Balcary Point, Balcary Hill and The Tower.

broad rocky bay, fringed with conifer. After enjoying the view of the crashing waves and the bay sweeping round to Castle Muir Point to the west, follow the path down to the left past a few timbered houses to start the return walk. A good path leads between steep earth cliffs with occasional outcrops of rock and the stony beach and the sea.

The tremendous cliffs at Balcary Point.

After a while the path rises from the shore to skirt the clifftop above the sea-eroded wave-cut platform of Adam's Chair. Looking back, the view has opened out beyond Castle Muir Point and you can see Abbey Head in the distance. Airds Point is soon reached with its wave-battered rock pinnacles and impressive yellow lichen-covered cliffs, sheer to the sea.

Traverse the hillside, there is another hill fort on the summit up and to the left, and you arrive at a junction with a stile and gate. It is possible to return to the Balcary Bay Hotel via the path on the left, but this misses out some of the most dramatic cliff scenery on the route.

From here the path rises up onto Balcary Heughs and goes quite close to the cliffs, so care should be taken, especially in wet weather and with young children. On a blustery day the sea pinnacles – one called Lot's Wife – whirling seabirds and precipitous cliffs will leave a lasting impression. Continue up and over the side of Balcary Hill and Hestan Island appears with Criffel behind. Slightly lower down there is a bench and a large sea pinnacle where it is easy to stop and admire the view for a while.

The path then drops down into a more sheltered area of gorse and enters the woodland that protects The Tower near the point. This path continues through woodland and past a boathouse and garden to emerge at a stile and open fields. Cross the field, taking in the fine view down right to Balcary Bay and the hotel beyond, to a gate and stile beside the house in the far right-hand corner. From here a path leads back to the road and the car-park. Turning right on the road will take you down to the bay and a pleasant view of the hotel, Hestan Island and The Tower on the point.

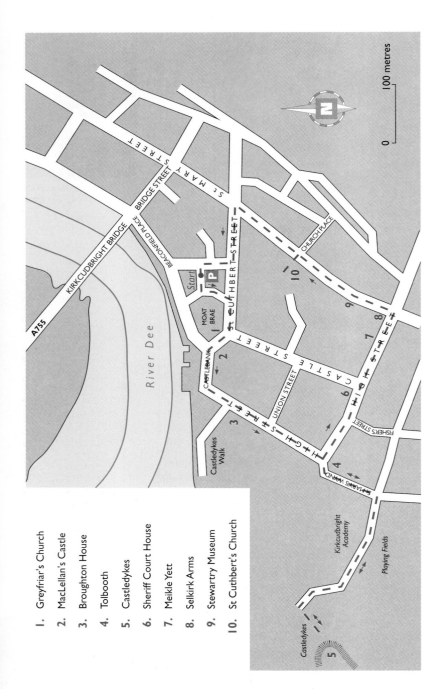

1. Greyfriar's Church
2. MacLellan's Castle
3. Broughton House
4. Tolbooth
5. Castledykes
6. Sheriff Court House
7. Meikle Yett
8. Selkirk Arms
9. Stewartry Museum
10. St Cuthbert's Church

100 metres

KIRKCUDBRIGHT

Kirkcudbright, pronounced Kir-coo-bree, is thought to originate from Cuthbert's Kirk. Certainly, Bede narrates in *The Life of St Cuthbert* how Cuthbert visited the land of the Niduari or Picts of Galloway who were then under the domination of the Picts of Northumbria.

The town appears to have been well established by the 12th century, defended by marshy ground to the east of the present Castle Street and a ditch and wall round the south and west sides of the High Street with two gates.

Whatever its origins, Kirkcudbright has a long history, much of which can still be seen, and is the outstanding historic town of the region. Over the years it has attracted artists and writers to its gentle streets, and continues to do so today. As just one example, the crime writer Dorothy L. Sayers wrote *Five Red Herrings* in Kirkcudbright in 1931.

INFORMATION

Distance: 2km (1¼ miles)

Start and Finish: Harbour Square car-park

Terrain: Paths and pavements. No special footwear needed.

Map: Town maps available in local shops and at the Tourist Information Centre.

Refreshments: Kirkcudbright has full facilities.

Opening hours: *The Tourist Information Office* at the harbour car-park is open daily, 1000–1700. *Broughton House:* Easter, 1 May–24 Oct., daily, 1300–1730. Admission charge. *Stewartry Museum:* Mar.-Oct.: Mon-Sat, 1100–1600 (Jul.-Aug. 1000–1800), plus Jun.-Sep., Sun 1400–1700. Nov.-Feb., Sat only, 1000–1600. Admission charge. *Wildlife Park:* Kirkcudbright near Lochfergus, 1.5 km east of Kirkcudbright on the B727, is signposted from the town.

Kirkcudbright harbour.

This walk starts at the Harbour Square car-park located on an infilled boat dock built around 1817 over a tidal creek. The River Dee has a high tidal rise and as late as 1844 Lord Cockburn described the town as the 'Venice of Scotland'. The harbour was important to the town for centuries – the 7th Lord Maxwell conspired with Philip II of Spain for Kircudbright to have been a landing place for the Spanish Armada in 1588 – but the old harbour has long gone.

Kirkcudbright.

Straight ahead is the present small harbour with its fleet of fishing boats, and to the left, the raised mound of Moat Brae topped with Greyfriar's Church. The church incorporates the remains of a Franciscan Friary including the tomb of Sir Thomas MacLellan and his wife Grissell Maxwell, erected in 1597.

Across the way is the substantial ruined tower house, better known as MacLellan's Castle after its builder Thomas MacLellan of Bombie. MacLellan married

Dame Grissell Maxwell, daughter of the powerful Lord
Herries and the 'castle', although built in the
traditional defensive style in 1582, is more the grand

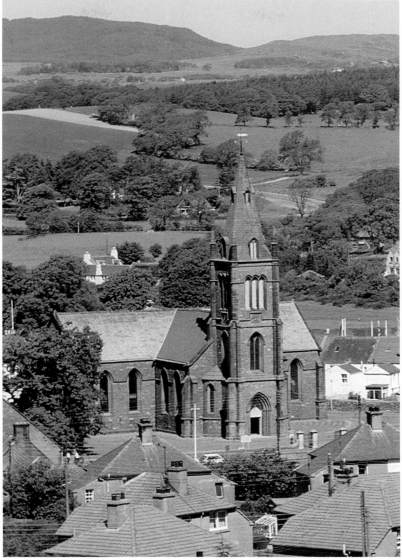

St. Cuthbert's Church,
Kirkcudbright.

town house of a wealthy man. Alas, the family's
support of the Royalist cause during the English Civil
War and escapades in Ireland cost them dear. Between
1664 and 1669 the estates were seized by creditors and
in 1752 the roof and internal fittings were stripped out.

Continue right into Castle Bank. On the left is Auchengool House, mentioned in the Burgh records of 1617 and possibly one of the oldest occupied houses in the town. Walk round into the High Street. The fine Georgian houses lining this L-shaped street give it an elegant air. Down and on the right is Broughton House, built by John Murray. It was the home of the artist E. A. Hornel from 1909 to 1910 and was left to the people of Kirkcudbright when he died in 1933. The house and garden recently passed into the care of the National Trust for Scotland. It is open to the public and has an impressive collection of 'Burnsiana' as well as the fine Hornel paintings.

The High Street is dominated by the characterful Tolbooth building that faces down the street from its southerly end. The main part of the building (there have been many additions and alterations over the years) was constructed between 1625–27 as a tolbooth and prison-house – the top row of small windows were the cells. The original clock, installed in 1642, is now in the Stewartry Museum and the ship weathervane is said to commemorate the Battle of Trafalgar in 1805. The Tolbooth now houses an art centre.

Walk round the building to the right, noticing the 'jougs' or iron manacles hanging from the corner of the Tolbooth, and enter St Mary's Wynd. Walk down the wynd and turn right down a small road with Kirkcudbright Academy on the right and playing fields on the left. Shortly after passing a white cottage on the left the road opens out into parkland. Over on the left is the Castledykes.

This mass of mounds and ditches is all that remains of Kirkcudbright's royal castle. Over to the right is a large sandstone block with a plaque. The castle is thought to have been built by Alexander III of Scotland in 1264, coming under the sheriffdom of John Comyn in 1288, and passing to the English in 1291 when Edward I placed it in the hands of the Scottish 'puppet king' John Balliol (see also Walks 8 and 19). Edward invaded Galloway in 1300 in the wake of William

Wallace's uprising, bringing with him 6000 men and 60 ships, and stayed in the castle.

By the time of Robert the Bruce's uprising of 1306 the castle was used as an English supply base and was probably laid siege to, as with Caerlaverock. By 1500 the castle was being used as a quarry and by 1577 it had all but gone. Excavation in 1911–13 revealed the size of the castle, wet moat and double-towered north-east facing gatehouse.

Return to the Tolbooth and continue down the High Street past the Sheriff Court House on the left with its dominating steeple. After passing Castle Street on your left you pass the brightly coloured facades of the council offices and a plaque on the railings which states that the two stones set into the road at that point mark the site of the Meikle Yett (the town gate).

On the left-hand side, on the corner of St Mary's Street, is the Selkirk Arms, which was built about 1750. Robert Burns stayed here a number of times when visiting the Earl of Selkirk on St Mary's Isle. The inn was called the Heid Inn at that time, and tradition has it that he delivered the 'Selkirk Grace' first at the inn on the afternoon of 1st August 1793, rather than later that evening on St Mary's Isle.

Turn left down St Mary Street and the Stewartry Museum is down on the left. It has a fine collection of objects relating to the history of the Stewartry of Kircudbright. Further down the street, pass by St Cuthbert's Church built in 1838 and then turn left along St Cuthbert Street back to the car.

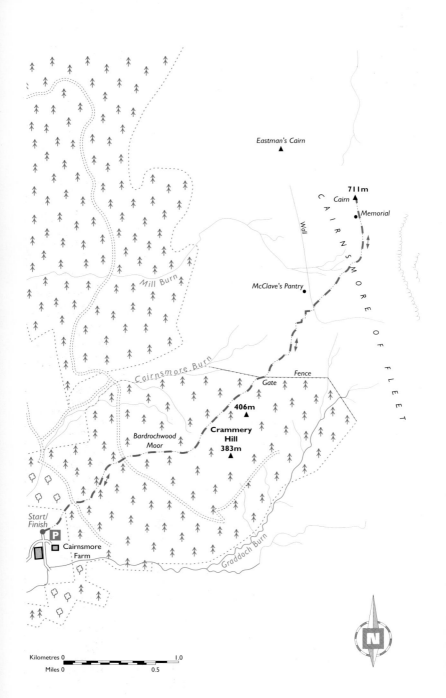

Eastman's Cairn

711m

Cairn

Memorial

C A I R N S M O R E

Wall

McClave's Pantry

O F

Mill Burn

Cairnsmore Burn

Fence

Gate

F L E E T

406m

**Crammery
Hill
383m**

Bardrochwood
Moor

Graddoch Burn

*Start/
Finish*

P

Cairnsmore
Farm

N

Kilometres 0   1.0
Miles 0   0.5

CAIRNSMORE OF FLEET

Despite its impressive mass and highly respectable 711 m, Cairnsmore of Fleet (part of the Cairnsmore of Fleet National Nature Reserve) is actually one of the more straightforward hill walks in this book. To a great extent this is due to the excellent path that winds its way up the western flanks of the mountain from the farm at Cairnsmore.

It's one of three hills in the region with the name Cairnsmore. An old rhyme says:

Cairnsmore o' Fleet and Cairnsmore o' Dee,
And Cairnsmore o' Carsphairn, the biggest o' the three.

Cairnsmore of Carsphairn, 797 m, lies north of Carsphairn on the A713 Dalmellington to St John's Town of Dalry road and is easily seen from Benbrack (Walk 16). An ascent is quite straightforward, but isn't described in this book. Cairnsmore or Black Craig of Dee is a lowly 493 m and lies south of the A712 New Galloway to Newton Stewart road, just east of Clatteringshaws Loch.

So Cairnsmore of Fleet isn't the highest, but it has something the others lack; an inspiring outlook over the flat, fertile plains of the River Cree to Wigtown Bay. Like so much of the coastal plain overlooking the Solway Firth, people have been living and farming here since the Stone Age, around 3000 to 4000BC.

INFORMATION

Distance: 9.5 km (6 miles).

Start and Finish: Cairnsmore Farm. Leave the A75 at the white farmhouse of Muirfad (GR 457629), 5 km east of Newton Stewart, near where the road crosses the River Cree on a bridge and where power-lines cross the road. At the viaduct; take the railinged gate on the right signposted 'Cairnsmore Estate'. The road then follows the burn, crosses it, and passes Cairnsmore house on the left. Approach a white building, which looks like a former coach house, take a sharp turn to the left and continue straight for a short distance to a cross roads. Turn left and park on the left a short way down the track, by a couple of picnic tables.

Terrain: Stout footwear, adequate waterproofs and warm clothing are recommended. A map and compass should always be carried, even though the paths are good.

Map: OS Landranger sheet 83, Newton Stewart & Kirkcudbright area.

Refreshments: Shops, pubs and cafes at Newton Stewart and Creetown and an *Information Centre* at Newton Stewart.

Other Activities: Creetown has an interesting gem museum. The Stone Age chambered cairns at Cairnholy (GR 517538) to the south of Creetown are some of the finest examples in Scotland.

Cairnsmore of Fleet and Craignelder, left, seen from the west near Wigtown.

The evidence is clear to see on any map. Standing stones, cup and ring marked rocks, cairns and chambered cairns litter the land. Some are particularly worth visiting, especially Cairnholy (GR 518539), just off the A75 about 12 km south of Cairnsmore of Fleet.

Cairnsmore of Fleet has another, rather sadder attraction. Between 1940 and 1944 no fewer than eight aircraft crashed into the mountain and the crews, from Canada, UK, New Zealand and Holland are now remembered in a memorial plaque near the summit. The plaque also pays tribute to two USAF crew killed in a Phantom jet in 1979. The area remains very popular for low-level flying by the RAF. A certain amount of wreckage still litters the summit – a characteristic of many peaks in the Galloway area.

Cairnsmore of Fleet flanked by the superb standing stones at Drumtroddan, west of Whithorn (see also Walk 22).

From the parking area, walk to the gate at the end of the track, cross the field past hawthorn bushes diagonally to go through a metal gate in the very top left-hand corner of the field. Cross a stile into an area of silver birch, holly, rowan, oak and rhododendrons and then into the modern Glenure Forest plantation. After a few minutes you emerge onto more open land surrounded by a much younger plantation. Some height has already been gained and it's worth looking back to green fields, the River Cree and the estuary and the distinctive top of Craigeach Fell, 131 m.

Cross over a forestry track and continue until after a while the path, which by now has become obvious and well worn, cuts over to the left-hand side heading towards the rounded top of the mountain up and on your left. If you look back halfway along this traversing path you can see the Mull of Galloway, and 'floating offshore' on the left-hand side above the estuary, the hills of the Isle of Man.

Eventually emerge onto open moorland. Cross a wall and continue to where the path levels out left onto the top of the plateau, from where cairns are followed off to the left. After a short time you reach the polished granite memorial stone to the fallen airmen. A short distance on from the stone is the trig point and the remains of an old building and on the left a cairn which appears higher than the trig point. It's worth a short walk north-west from the top for the view down to Murray's Monument above the A712 west of Clatteringshaws Loch. Below Eastman's Cairn (GR 495675) are various aircraft remains.

A short detour on the descent is a visit to small cave called McClave's Pantry. Start from the wall which crosses the path below the summit slope. The cave lies among the outcrop of boulders just below the wall and north of the path. Follow the downhill side of the wall north-west for about 10 minutes and then descend about 200 paces to the cave. It is well marked by a cairn above, and is about 2 m long, a metre wide and just over a metre high.

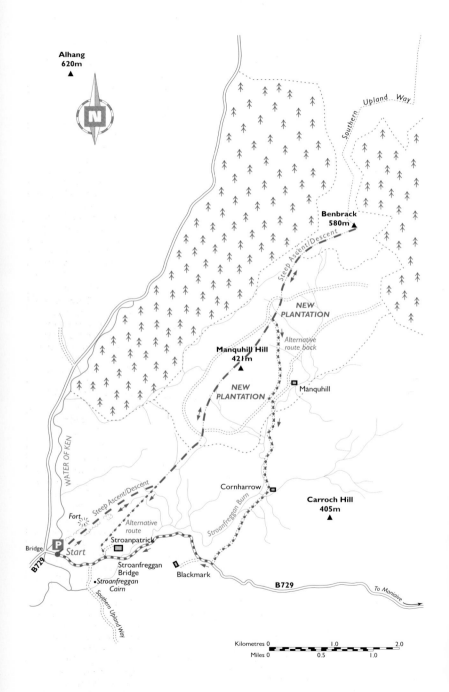

Alhang
620m
▲

N

Southern Upland Way

Benbrack
580m ▲

Steep Ascent/Descent

NEW
PLANTATION

Alternative
route back

Manquhill Hill
421m
▲

NEW
PLANTATION

Manquhill

WATER OF KEN

Steep Ascent/Descent

Cornharrow

Carroch Hill
405m
▲

Fort

Alternative
route

Stroanpatrick

Stroanfreggan Burn

Bridge

P
Start

B729

Stroanfreggan
Bridge

Stroanfreggan
Cairn

Blackmark

B729

To Moniaive

Southern Upland Way

Kilometres 0   1.0   2.0
Miles 0   0.5   1.0

BENBRACK

The Southern Upland Way was officially opened on 27 April 1984 and winds its way for 340 km (212 miles) across Scotland from Portpatrick on the west coast to Cockburnspath on the east. It crosses a wide variety of upland and lowland terrain, forms part of three walks in this book (see Walks 1 and 19) and passes close to others.

Much of this walk to the summit of Benbrack and back follows the Southern Upland Way. However, unconstrained by the Way's need for a 'straight' route, we are free to start our walk with an ascent of the considerably drier and slightly more interesting ridge below Stroanfreggan Craig to the west.

Cross over the gate and ascend the hillside towards the large and ancient cairn. Unlike the boggy start to the Southern Upland Way beyond Stroanpatrick, the ground underfoot is firm and dry. The view up the wide and forest-clad Water of Ken is very fine. On the left Cairnsmore of Carsphairn, Beninner and Moorbrock Hill dominate the view with the smaller Windy Standard in the distance at the head of the glen. The land round here has been farmed for thousands of years, a statement easily backed up by the concentration of ancient remains marked on the map; Neolithic burial mounds, a Bronze Age cairn, Iron Age fort, and a Mesolithic hunting camp.

The Iron Age fort is reached first, in a commanding position high on the ridge above the confluence of the

Towards Cairnsmore of Carsphairn and the Water of Ken from Stroanfreggan Cairn.

INFORMATION

Distance: (10 miles), or 18 km (11½ miles) if returning via Cornharrow and the road.

Start and Finish: Beside the bridge over the Water of Ken. From Carsphairn on A713 take B729 and in 6 km turn left at the junction (still B729). In 2.5 km, cross the bridge over the Water of Ken and park tidily on the right or a short way up the track on the left that leads to a small quarry at the base of the ridge.

Terrain: Open hillside which can be tough, wet and tiring on the feet. Strong footwear, waterproofs, map and compass essential. Most of the route is waymarked with Southern Upland Way marker posts.

Map: OS Landranger sheet 77, Dalmellington to New Galloway.

Refreshments: Carsphairn has a hotel, shops and a post office. Toilets at Carsphairn Heritage Centre.

Opening hours: *Carsphairn Heritage Centre* has a permanent exhibition of village crafts and skills from the last century. Open Mon-Sat except Wed 1030–1700, Sun 1400-1700, Easter week, 30 May-30 Sept. and the October half-term week. Weekends only from 1 April-29 May (except Easter week) and in October.

Water of Ken and the Stroanfreggan Burn; fallen walls surround a central enclosure. The route continues uphill on the edge of some small crags, passing to the right of a small plantation. At the top of the hill the route can be surveyed. Ahead is another small plantation of conifer with a rowan tree and an aspen down to its right. Beyond are the ploughed ridges of recently-planted Manquhill Hill, just shielding the distant Benbrack from view.

Descend from the hilltop and pass to the left of most of the fields to pass to the right of the small plantation

and above the rowan tree. At this point a short descent down towards the sheep pens on the right will link up with the Southern Upland Way markers above the wall. With Cairnsmore of Carsphairn hidden behind the ridge to the north, the eye is drawn south-

Looking back towards the Rhinns of Kells while following the wall below Manquhill Hill.

westwards as you ascend, to the Rhinns of Kells and to their left Curlywee and Cairnsmore of Fleet. Unfortunately, south-west Scotland has one of the highest military presences in Britain and it is not unusual to have your quiet admiration of the landscape shattered by the explosive roar of a low flying jet.

Follow the path beside the wall for almost a kilometre, rising gradually, but still quite boggy in places, and cross a stile at the junction of two walls. To the north Cairnsmore of Carsphairn has started to appear once more. This path brings you round to the right where the view opens up ahead towards the western Nithsdale valleys. Cross a forestry access track and follow the waymarks on the other side along a section of specially made path aiming towards the top of Manquhill Hill.

This track leads on to the shoulder below the hill and then skirts the summit to the north. A short diversion to the summit is well worth while for the panorama of hills to the north and west and the view of Benbrack's broad flanks to the east. Much of this area has been recently planted and although at the time of writing the trees are mere saplings, it will not be long before this open moorland landscape is transformed.

Descend towards the col between the two hills and pick

A snow covered Cairnsmore of Carsphairn from the small bridge over the Water of Deugh between Marscalloch and Knowehead.

up the waymarks again. Cross a forestry track before the col and pass beside some artificial ponds. They were created by the local Rangers service, funded by SNH to add some variety for walkers on the way. Start climbing uphill again and cross a second forestry track before the path leads onto the open Shoulder of Corlae and a steady climb to the trig point on the broad summit of Benbrack.

To the east of Benbrack is Cairnkinna (Walk 3) and well to the south, Criffel and the sea.

There are three options for the return walk. The first is by the way of ascent, back onto the ridge above Stroanfreggan fort. It is also possible to return this way to the small plantation and the rowan tree, and then to continue left on the Way to Stroanpatrick followed by a short walk down the main road to the car. This also allows a quick look at the Stroanfreggan cairn, situated on the left before the bridge, a short way down the track where the Way leaves the main road. Unfortunately, the cairn has little shape left and looks like any other pile of stones. The large boulder in the centre covers an oblong cist which revealed a stone knife when excavated in 1910.

The last option is to return to the col between Manquhill Hill and Benbrack and pick up the forestry track to descend south to the bothy at Manquhill and then on to the house at Cornharrow and thus to the road. The road is then descended back to the car. This route is interesting but involves a fair amount of track and road walking and can be quite tough on the feet as a result.

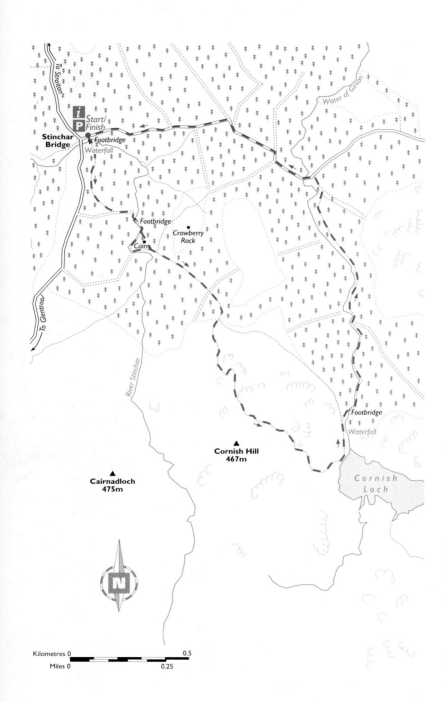

To Straiton

Water of Girvan

ℹ️ Start/ Finish

Stinchar Bridge

Footbridge

Waterfall

To Glentroo/

Footbridge

Cairn

Crawberry Rock

River Stinchar

Footbridge

Waterfall

▲ Cornish Hill 467m

Cornish Loch

▲ Cairnadloch 475m

N

Kilometres 0   0.5

Miles 0   0.25

CORNISH HILL AND LOCH

This Forestry Commission waymarked route is one of the shorter hill walks in this book and gives a good introduction to walking in the Galloway hills, with a combination of gentle sheltered forest walking and more open rugged hillside.

At 467 m, Cornish Hill is quite small, but the views of Ayrshire's western coastline, Cairnsmore of Carsphairn to the east and the impressive flanks of Shalloch on Minnoch and Merrick to the south are unexpectedly good. A visit to Cornish Hill will help the visitor mentally 'colour in' the northern aspect of this fine mountain area, without excessive effort.

Following one of the well-maintained Forestry Commission woodchip paths through the forest below Cornish Loch.

INFORMATION

Distance: 5 km (3 miles).

Start and Finish: Car-park at Stinchar Bridge. From Straiton, 10 km west of Dalmellington on B41, head south on the old minor road between Straiton and Glentrool Village. In 10 km when you arrive at the bridge, turn left, marked 'Forestry Commission Stinchar Falls Loch Bradan', continue uphill then immediately left up a track to a car-park.

Terrain: The forest paths are generally clean and dry. The section to Cornish Hill, down to Cornish Loch and alongside the Water of Girvan is marshy in places and suitable footwear is recommended. The forest sections are well waymarked and the section in open country has black and white marker posts.

Map: OS Landranger sheet 77, Dalmellington to New Galloway.

Refreshments: None, but the charming village of Straiton to the north has shops and a pub.

Other activities: A 10 km trail to Stinchar Falls, east of Stinchar Bridge is also possible. Fishing for brown trout is possible in Loch Bradan and Loch Skelloch with permits from the Forestry Commission. Cornish Loch is private and fishing is not permitted. The road at the end of the walk gives access to a forest drive to Loch Doon and is part of a larger cycle trail from Barr to Loch Doon.

Cornish Hill holds another special significance, for despite its modest height, it plays a crucial role in the life of two large Ayrshire rivers. The Water of Girvan rises above Loch Girvan Eye, high in the northern corrie of Shalloch on Minnoch

The view west towards the Ayr coast and the Island of Arran from the first viewpoint on the walk.

and flows into Cornish Loch, to the east of Cornish Hill, and then north and west to Girvan. The River Stinchar originates on Shalloch on Minnoch's northern side and flows to the west of Cornish Hill and then due west to the sea at Ballantrae. It is amusing to speculate that if Cornish Hill had been scoured away by the glaciers which formed this rugged mountain landscape, then the two rivers could have been one.

From the car-park, retrace your steps to the road; directions to the 'Cornish Loch Walk' point you across the road and left to a wooden bridge over the River Stinchar.

A very pleasant forest trail lined with wood chippings descends to another wooden bridge over the River Stinchar, from where a grassy path follows the left bank. A turning on the left leads to a cairn of stone blocks (marked on the OS map), or you can reach the same point by continuing alongside the burn.

As the woodchip path starts to rise through the conifer trees, Loch Bradan to the north comes into view, surrounded by the easterly plantations of the Carrick Forest.

In a short distance the gentle forest landscape is left for more rugged and open moorland – and more extensive views. The ground can be quite boggy in places but the route is well marked with black and white posts. In a short distance the summit of the first little hill gives extensive views west over the Ayrshire plain towards the mountainous profile of Arran and north to Loch Skelloch, Loch Bradan and Loch Finlas.

A short rise and the highest elevation of the walk is reached. The actual summit of Cornish Hill is a little off the path to the south, a slight diversion that is worthwhile, even just to experience the roughness of the off-path walking in the Galloway hills!

The view is quite startling. The hillside sweeps down to Cornish Loch, and then up to the retaining walls of Shiel Hill, 505 m, and the craggy mass of Craigmasheenie, 539 m, with the bulk of Cairnsmore of Carsphairn, 797 m, in the distance. To the right and further back is the imposing Shalloch on Minnoch, 768 m, with the flanks of Merrick, 843 m, behind.

Follow the marker posts easily to the loch and follow its edge to the outfall of the Water of Girvan a short distance to the north. At this point the marker posts head off left, back across the side of Cornish Hill, to return you to the point where you emerged from the forest on the ascent. However, it's more interesting to continue on the newly made path which follows the Water of Girvan back to the road.

Follow the burn through a small gorge and down rocky steps, to the obvious wooden bridge. Cross over and follow the right bank of the burn, with short diversions in and out of the conifer forest, created to avoid the marshier sections of the bank.

The view down towards Cornish Loch from Cornish Hill.

After some pleasant waterside wandering the path brings you out at the main road. Turn left and it's a short walk up the hill, then down to the car park from where you started.

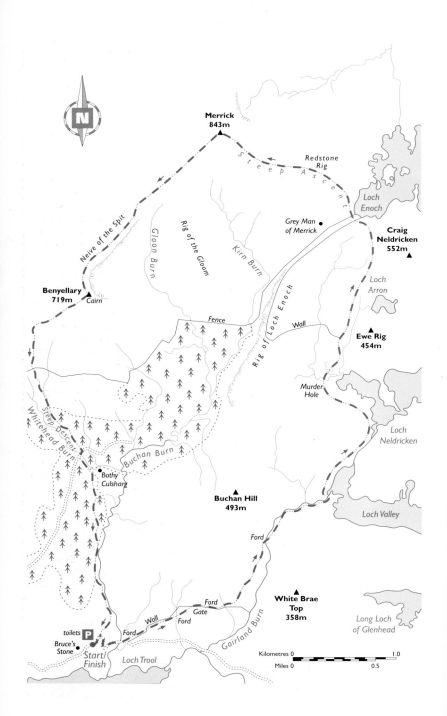

N

Merrick
843m

Steep Ascent

Redstone
Rig

Loch
Enoch

Neive of the Spit

Grey Man
of Merrick

Craig
Neldricken
552m

Gloon Burn

Rig of the Gloom

Kirn Burn

Loch
Arron

Benyellary
719m
Cairn

Fence

Wall

Rig of Loch Enoch

Ewe Rig
454m

Murder
Hole

Steep Descent

Whitehead Burn

Buchan Burn

Loch
Neldricken

Bothy
Culsharg

Buchan Hill
493m

Loch
Valley

Ford

White Brae
Top
358m

Long Loch
of Glenhead

Ford
Gate

Ford

Gairland Burn

Wall
Ford

toilets P

Bruce's
Stone

Start/
Finish

Loch Trool

Kilometres 0   1.0
Miles 0   0.5

MERRICK

The whale-backed bulk of Merrick dominates the hills round Loch Trool and offers a fine walk to the highest summit in the Galloway Hills. At 16 km it's one of the longest, and at 843 m the highest, walk in this book and much of the ground underfoot is quite rough, especially approaching via the four lochs. With that in mind a couple of variations are described to allow the walker some flexibility of route.

The standard approach from the Bruce's Stone car-park via the Buchan Burn and Whiteland Burn to the summit of Benyellary involves a long uphill section on muddy paths. A much more scenic route links the five lochs to the east of the hill and then climbs the east ridge to the summit. (See Walk 19, Loch Trool Circuit, for more information on Bruce's Stone).

Should time be short or the party a little slow then an ascent of Merrick via the Buchan Burn is recommended, or it is possible to tour the four lochs, leave the Merrick for another day and return over the Rig of Loch Enoch and Buchan Hill – a superb and satisfying walk in its own right.

To approach via the four lochs, descend the road from the Bruce's Stone car-park, towards the lodge. Cross over the bridge at the bottom, go past a sign for the Buchan Burn, and then cross the stile on the left and follow the signpost to Loch Valley and the Gairland Burn. The route crosses a field, often filled with sheep, and is quite indistinct in places. It is best to keep quite

INFORMATION

Distance: 16 km (10 miles) Four Lochs, Merrick, Benyellary. 13 km (8 miles) Four Lochs circuit. 13 km (8 miles) Benyellary, Merrick return.

Start and Finish: Bruce's Stone car-park on the north side of Loch Trool. From the A714 34 km south of Girvan, turn east and follow signs to the car park in 9 km.

Terrain: This is a mountain walk with some steep slopes and muddy paths. Stout boots, adequate waterproofs and warm clothing are essential and walkers are advised to be familiar with map and compass techniques. Sufficient food and drink should also be taken. Allow at least 6 hours.

Map: OS Landranger sheet 77, Dalmellington to New Galloway.

Refreshments: *Glen Trool Visitor Centre* (GR 372786), has a good cafe and small shop. Open Easter-end Oct daily, 1030-1730. There are toilets here and at the Bruce's Stone car-park.

Loch Trool from Buchan Hill.

high on the hillside until you reach a gate in the wall at the top of the field.

Cross over the gate and follow the, by now, much more distinct path alongside the delightful Gairland Burn. The path rises to the outflow from Loch Valley. The quality of the path is good, but it can be a bit wet in places. From the outflow follow the side of the surprisingly long Loch Valley on a continuously good path which then rises to the outfall of Loch Neldricken.

Walk round the loch on the left on an indistinct path and cross a wall by the 'Murder Hole'. This area of deep water at the westerly end of the loch is featured in S. R. Crockett's novel of cattle rustling and murder, *The Raiders*, and is said to never freeze over.

Follow a wall rising up Ewe Rig to the smaller Loch Arron. From here continue upwards alongside one of

the small burns that cleft the hillside. This will bring you out at a small col overlooking Loch Enoch and the hump of Mullwharchar behind. Incidentally, the name of this hill is thought to derive

Mullwharchar and boulder strewn granite pavement above Loch Enoch.

from the Gaelic, Maol Adhairce, meaning Hill of the Huntsman's Horn. It's worth spending a few minutes soaking up the views across to Merrick and Redstone Rig, the line of ascent. Although only four lochs are visited, five can be seen as the largest island on Loch Enoch has a loch of its own! Go down to the sandy loch shore and some splendid lunch spots. Follow the shore round, crossing a wall and then a fence.

A small diversion is possible at this point to the 'Grey Man of Merrick' (GR 437846), if time allows. Follow the fence a short way down, keeping to its right, and up on the right is a small crag. When viewed from the north, part of the cliff looks like a face.

If time is pressing it is possible to descend past the 'Grey Man' beside the Buchan Burn (some ascent and descent), or to climb up onto the Rig of Loch Enoch and follow this via Buchan Hill (quite rough) back to the car-park. If a completely downhill alternative is desired, you can retrace your steps beside the lochs.

To ascend Merrick, retrace your steps and follow the long haul up Redstone Rig. Thankfully the hillside isn't too steep, but it's steep enough to be tiring. Don't rush this bit as it's quite long and although the descent from the summit is almost all downhill, it is still quite a long way. Just as the hillside looks like it will never end it starts to level out and the summit trig point can be seen a short distance away.

From the summit the view makes all the hard work worthwhile; there are open views to Craignaw in the east, the broad ridge of Tarfessock and Shalloch of Minnoch to the north and Mulldonnoch and Lamachan Hill to the south, with the four lochs sparkling below.

Looking back along the Neive of the Spit towards the summit of Merrick.

From the summit a pleasant and gradually descending path contours the Neive of the Spit towards Benyellary and the mast on the summit of Bennan. Benyellary, or Benyellarie as it used to be spelt, derives from the Gaelic for 'the eagle's hill'.

After crossing over Benyellary follow the path down and left and over a stile and then down beside the Whiteland Burn. This section of the descent is quite steep. From the bottom you arrive at Culsharg bothy. From there follow the path and often very muddy forestry track south alongside the Buchan Burn back to the car-park.

To approach Merrick from the car-park, follow the signposted path and the previous directions in reverse. Return the same way or descend to Loch Enoch and return to the car-park via the 'Grey Man' and the Buchan Burn, or Rig of Loch Enoch and Buchan Hill.

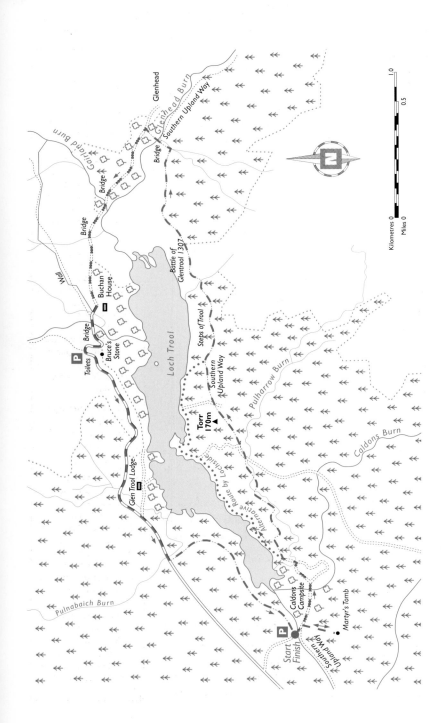

Glenhead

Garroch Burn

Bridge

Glenhead Burn

Southern Upland Way

Bridge

Bridge

Wall

Buchan House

Bridge

Battle of Glentrool 1307

Steps of Trool

P

Toilets

Bruce's Stone

Loch Trool

Southern Upland Way

Torr 170m ▲

Pulharrow Burn

Caldons Burn

Glen Trool Lodge

Alternative Route by Lochside

Pulnabaich Burn

Caldons Campsite

Martyr's Tomb

P

Start Finish

Southern Upland Way

Kilometres 0   0.5   1.0

Miles 0

N

LOCH TROOL CIRCUIT

The combination of Glen Trool's winding tree-fringed loch and craggy hillsides of dappled greens and browns is always enriching, in the way that similar landscapes in the Trossachs and the English Lake District have inspired artists and writers for generations. Today it is a gentle place for a lowland walk, but its past encapsulates two quite different periods of violence in the political and religious struggle between Scotland and England.

The late 13th century was marked by internal disputes over succession to the Scottish crown and Edward I of England's determination to retain influence over the Anglo-Norman claimants, and maintain their allegiance to the English throne. Edward chose John Balliol, rejecting John Comyn the elder and Robert Bruce the elder. But Balliol's rule ended in chaos and the Tower of London and the crown passed into the guardianship of, among others, Robert Bruce the younger (better known as Robert the Bruce).

This disorder led to the first real move for Scottish independence from the Scottish knight William Wallace. After a number of campaigns, supported by, among others, Robert the Bruce, Wallace was defeated, captured by Edward I and beheaded in London in 1305. By this time Bruce had married into the English royal family, been pardoned for his part in the rebellion, taken a place at the English court and been appointed to the advisory council ruling Scotland in lieu of a monarch. But Bruce's ambition drove him on.

The event that put him on the road to the throne took place in Dumfries in 1306 (see Walk 6) when Bruce murdered fellow claimant and advisory council member John 'the Red' Comyn. Events moved fast with Bruce and his followers attacking and seizing the nearby English garrison at Castledykes. After being crowned king at Scone, Bruce was defeated by the English at Methven and fled to Ireland, where he is said to have encountered the famous spider in a cave on Rathlin Island.

INFORMATION

Distance: 5 km (3 miles).

Start and Finish: Caldons camp site car park, Glen Trool. From A714 34 km south of Girvan at Bargrennan, turn east and follow signs to the car park in 6 km. Park in the first car-park on the left or at Stroan Bridge.

Terrain: Generally good forest paths and tracks, but can be rough and muddy. Strong footwear is recommended. Most of the path on the south bank of the loch has Southern Upland Way waymarks. Various signs on the north side.

Map: OS Landranger sheet 77, Dalmellington and New Galloway.

Refreshments: Caldons camp site shop: Mon-Sat, 0900–1200, 1330–1600, 1800–1900. Sun, 0930–1200, 1330–1600. Sells sweets, assorted food, drinks and OS maps. Toilets. Toilets also available at the car-park beside Bruce's Stone.

Opening Hours: Glen Trool Visitor Centre (GR372786), has a good cafe and small shop. Open Easter-end Oct daily, 1030–1730. Toilets.

Returning home in 1307, his first tangle with the English was at Raploch Moss (see Walk 21). On 31 March in the same year he gained a more impressive victory on the shores of Glen Trool after tricking an English force under Clifford into an ambush. Bruce's war of independence ended with final victory over Edward II at Bannockburn in 1314.

This walk round Loch Trool starts at the Caldons camp site at the west end of the loch, signposted from the lochside road. Cross over the bridge, the car-park on the right has information on the battle of the Steps of Glen Trool and the Covenanters (see later), and follow the road into the camp site. A signpost on the right gives directions to the Martyr's Tomb, a short distance into the Caldons Wood.

The Martyr's Tomb near Caldons camp site at the start of the walk.

The 1558 Reformation marked the start of a political struggle between church and state that was to last for many years. The Presbyterian system established in Scotland removed the power to appoint church ministers from the king and made the church an independent and often critical voice.

James VI and his son Charles I tried to establish an Episcopal system similar to the Anglican church today. In 1638 the Scots set up a National Covenant of Protest from which the word Covenanter comes. On his restoration to the throne in 1660, Charles II caused non-conforming ministers to be removed, and these ministers held open air services or Conventicles, attendance at which became an offence punishable by death.

In the large walled enclosure in Caldons Wood are stones commemorating the execution of six 'martyrs' on 25 January 1685.

The inscribed centre stone is a copy of one erected by the mason-engraver Robert 'Old Mortality' Patterson (1712–1800), who dedicated his life to the maintenance and re-inscription of memorials to the victims of Scotland's 'Killing Times' (see Walk 6, Dumfries).

Return to the road and follow it to the shop in the middle of the site, and then take the road on the left towards the loch. Where it curves back right a rough track, signposted with a thistle logo and green waymark (this is part of the Southern Upland Way long distance path) points left over a small bridge to a large oak tree.

From here two routes are possible. You can continue down the track and follow a path along the edge of the loch, or the waymarked route on the right. The waymarked route is very obvious, the lochside path less so and rougher, although more interesting and scenic. The lochside route is marked on the Western Section of the special OS/HMSO 1:50,000 maps to *The Southern Upland Way* guide.

Either way, both paths lead through old and airy plantations of Scots pine, silver fir and larch, to link together beyond the spur opposite Glen Trool Lodge on the north side of the loch. The section along the flanks of Mulldonoch, where the English army was ambushed, is rough and quite rocky, so care should be taken. An information board marks the approximate location of the battle.

The path continues above the area of flat land at the head of the loch and

The bridge over the Glenhead Burn at Glenhead.

down to a bridge over the Glenhead Burn. The path then joins the track from Glenhead which leads west through old woodland, and uphill to the car-park at Bruce's Stone, which commemorates the 1307 victory.

Continue along the road below the Fell of Eschoncan, devastated by a fire in the very dry spring of 1994, until past Glen Trool Lodge where a path signposted with a green waymark, leaves the road on the left-hand side just after a small burn on the right. Follow the path down to a small bridge, enter the forest and follow the path back to the camp site.

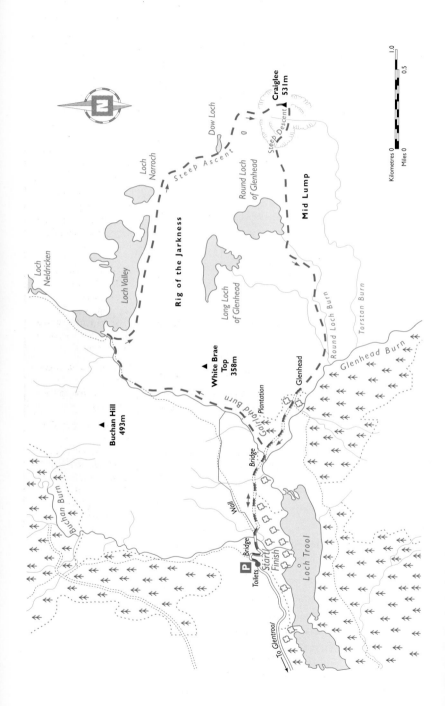

Craiglee 531m

Dow Loch

Steep Descent

Steep Ascent

0

Loch Narroch

Round Loch of Glenhead

Mid Lump

Rig of the Jarkness

Loch Neldricken

Loch Valley

Long Loch of Glenhead

Round Loch Burn

Torstan Burn

White Brae Top 358m

Gairland Burn

Glenhead Burn

Buchan Hill 493m

Glenhead

Gairland Plantation

Bridge

Buchan Burn

Wall

Bridge

Start Finish

Loch Trool

P

Toilets

To Glentrool

Kilometres 0   1.0

Miles 0   0.5

N

CRAIGLEE

Craiglee is a secretive little hill, separated from the main range to the north by its long west ridge, the poetically named Rig of the Jarkness and the long Loch Valley. It is quite a rough walk for such a small hill.

With a pair of binoculars the summit trig point (531 m) can actually be seen from the car-park at the Bruce's Stone, a small pimple near the end of the long, brown ridge above the continuation of the road, eastwards.

At first glance it isn't a particularly interesting mountain, but it is the hidden delights, the Long Loch and Round Loch of Glenhead, nestling in the granite bowl below the summit and the scattered lochs and pools on the Rig of Jarkness, that make an ascent of this hill so worthwhile.

From the Bruce's Stone walk towards the lodge, and continue down the track for about 15 minutes to a wooden bridge crossing the Gairland Burn in a small deciduous wood. Turn left and follow the right bank of the burn via a vague path which peters out here and there. After leaving the small wood it gets quite wet underfoot in places.

Skirt a small conifer plantation on the left, then cross the wall at an obvious gap and follow the fence left to where the barbed wire ends beside the burn.

From here there are superb views back to Loch Trool and Glen Trool. Gairland Burn is particularly impressive when there's plenty of water in it, creating lots of small waterfalls as it cascades, sparkling in the sun down granite slabs and over piles of blocks. It's hardly surprising that the name Gairland – pronounced Ghairland – derives from Gaelic meaning rough pool or a rapid stream forming many cascades.

The burn soon opens out into a wide, rather barren, colourless glen, a surprising landscape after the richness of the cascades. The ground is quite marshy underfoot

INFORMATION

Distance: 13 km (8 miles)

Start and Finish: Bruce's Stone car-park on the north side of Loch Trool. For directions see walk 18.

Terrain: Craiglee is a small hill, but it still has some steep slopes and muddy footpaths. Stout boots, adequate waterproofs and warm clothing are recommended and walkers are advised to be familiar with map and compass techniques. Sufficient food and drink should also be taken. Allow at least 4 hours.

Map: OS Landranger sheet 77, Dalmellington to New Galloway.

Refreshments: *Glen Trool Visitor Centre* (GR 372786), has a good cafe and small shop. Open Easter-end Oct, daily 1030–1730. There are toilets here and at the Bruce's Stone car-park.

Looking down the Gairland Burn towards Glen Trool.

in places and it's best sticking to the sheep tracks beside the burn. At the top of the glen the landscape opens out again, but keep following the burn on its right-hand side. Before Loch Valley is a little hill, part of the glacial moraines that retain the lochs, which can be turned by following the burn on the left (rough) or via the obvious path right, away from the burn. Both routes soon arrive at the shore of Loch Valley.

The next section is worth taking time over. There is an obvious path, most of which is quite straightforward, but one section near the end involves crossing some grass-covered boulders with holes between them and requires a little care. Continue wandering round the side of the loch past lots of little sandy bays. About halfway round the loch a superb perched granite boulder on a plinth can be seen, high up on the flanks of Rig of the Jarkness above the path.

The path is never more than a few feet above the loch and even on a day with only a little breeze, the sound of water lapping onto the granite boulders is never far away. As you progress there are fine views back to Merrick and the sweeping saddleback ridge of Neive of the Spit which links it to Benyellary.

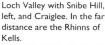

Loch Valley with Snibe Hill, left, and Craiglee. In the far distance are the Rhinns of Kells.

At the end of the surprisingly long Loch Valley, a small sandy beach makes a pleasant place for lunch.

Follow a fence east to the next loch – Loch Narroch –
and continue to the first gate just beside a big boulder
at the bottom of a large field of boulders on the left.

From here it is possible to zigzag straight up the north
side of Craiglee to arrive, in about 15 to 20 minutes,
on Rig of the Jarkness a little to the west of the small
Dow Loch. As you rise the view opens out above the
crags of Snibe Hill towards the Rhinns of Kells – Little
Millyea, Meikle Millyea and Millfore. In spring the
greenness of the conifers at the base of the Rhinns give
a strong contrast to the straw-coloured grass.

Once on the ridge, lots of small lochs and pools are
passed en route to the summit, still quite a long way
off. Glen Trool is revealed in all its beauty to the west,
but the two lochs of Glenhead remain largely hidden
until near the end. The final ridge is actually quite flat
with the summit and trig point
obvious in the distance. From the top
the view adds another piece to the
area's geographical jigsaw. To the
north are Merrick and the Rhinns of
Kells; to the east Loch Dee and
Clatteringshaws Loch away in the
distance with the Lake District
beyond; and to the south Millfore,
Curleywee, Lamachan Hill and Mulldonoch.

On the flanks of Craiglee
with Loch Narroch below
and Merrick behind.

Having taken your fill of the summit panorama, drop
straight down and follow a big grassy ramp southwards
until it is possible to move in a more north-westerly
direction towards the Round Loch of Glenhead,
which is now in sight. It is important to take some
time with this descent as the hillside is banded with
small granite crags between the ramps. However, all
are easily by-passed.

Descend to the Round Loch of Glenhead and follow
the left-hand side and then the right-hand side of the
Round Loch Burn which drains from the loch. This
leads to open fields beside Glenhead Farm. Pass
through a gate on the right into a field which leads to
the farmyard and the track leading back to the car park.

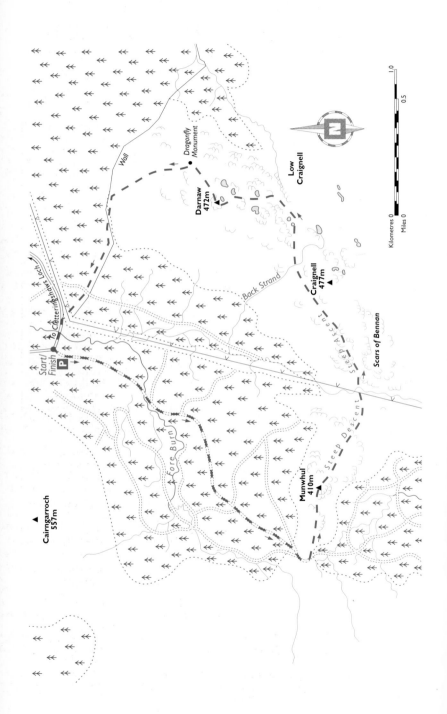

Cairngarroch
557m

Wall

Dragonfly
Monument

Darnaw
472m

Low
Craignell

Craignell
477m

Back Strand

Steep Ascent

Scars of Bennan

Steep Descent

Munwhul
410m

Fore Burn

Start/
Finish

P

To Clatteringshaws Loch

N

Kilometres 0   1.0
Miles 0   0.5

DARNAW AND THE DRAGONFLY MONUMENT

On Tuesday 2nd February 1937 a green 5-seater De Havilland aircraft took off from Renfrew Airport, Glasgow, and headed south. The destination of the *Daily Express* 'Dragonfly' was Liverpool. On board were Major Harold Pemberton DSO, the newspaper's motoring and air correspondent, *Daily Express* photographer Reginald Wesley, Archibald Philpott, a radio expert, and pilot Thomas Jackson from Croydon.

This was no ordinary flight. The plane had been touring the country surveying the routes suggested by a Parliamentary committee for a night air mail service, something Harold Pemberton had already described in the paper as 'suicidal' for aircraft without de-icers, a better rate of climb and night radio.

The weather over the Galloway hills that day was misty and wet and the plane never arrived, sparking the largest air search Britain had ever seen. Three days later the burned-out wreckage was found by shepherd Andrew Wilson on the flanks of Darnaw, embedded deep in the ground with its tail pointing to the sky and sheep grazing around. All on board died in the crash.

In many ways this is a sad story to be associated with such a beautiful area. However, every walker on Darnaw should visit the monument and in their own way pay tribute to the pilot and crew of a small plane which helped to pioneer the air routes which we take for granted.

The ascent of Darnaw is best accomplished from south of Craigencallie on the single-track road that skirts the west shore of Clatteringshaws Loch. Craigencallie, 'the old wife's crag', is reputed to be named after the woman who gave food and shelter to Robert the Bruce the night before the battle of Raploch Moss in 1307.

Cross over the stile and go left (south), making easy progress along the forest track with Darnaw up on the

INFORMATION

Distance: 9 km (5½ miles).

Start and Finish: At the gate south of Craigencallie. Leave the A712 10 km west of New Galloway at the no through road signposted 'Galloway Forest Park, Craignell and Lillie's Loch and Loch Dee'. After the road cuts inland from the loch go past pylons and over a narrow bridge to park on the left-hand side at a locked Forestry Commission gate with a couple of stiles. If the parking here is full, park at the gate below Craigencallie crag.

Terrain: Darnaw is a small hill, but the going is rough in places. Stout boots, adequate waterproofs and warm clothing are recommended and walkers are advised to be familiar with map and compass techniques.

Map: OS Landranger sheet 77, Dalmellington to New Galloway.

Refreshments: Clatteringshaws Forest Wildlife Centre.

Opening Hours: *Clatteringshaws Forest Wildlife Centre* (01644 420285) on the east bank of Clatteringshaws Loch is well worth a visit. Open Apr-Oct. daily 1000–1700; toilets, shop and cafe. Charge for parking.

left and good views of the craggy Buckdas of
Cairnbaber – from the Scandinavian bukkr dass, the
he-goat's ledge – and Millfore, 'the cold hill'. About a
half hour should bring you to a high point on the track
where the forest ends and the track starts to descend.
It's worth stopping here to take in the view south-east
to the bulk of Craignelder – 'the red hind's crag' – an
outlier of Cairnsmore of Fleet.

The Dragonfly monument
with Clatteringshaws Loch
behind.

Walk up on the left past some old quarry workings and
continue over rocky ground to the small cairn on the
top of Munwhul. From here it's straight down the
ridge towards the scree-strewn Scars of Bennan with
Craignell up on the right. Descend into the glen,
which has pylons running through it, climb out again
on the left-hand side between the screes and the
forestry plantation and head up and left, avoiding
Craignell, to the summit of Darnaw. The going is quite
steep and rough underfoot at this point.

On a fine day the summit of Darnaw is quite beautiful,
scattered with lochans filled with frogs' spawn in
spring. From the summit the panorama stretches from
Merrick, the Rhinns of Kells and Cairnsmore of
Carsphairn in the north to Clatteringshaws Loch and
the rounded contours of Cairnsmore of Dee in the
east, and Cairnsmore of Fleet and the sea to the south.

From the summit head north following the ridge
down, aiming towards the end of the Rhinns of Kells.

Traversing one of Darnaw's small lochs.

Make sure you keep well over to the right, as the Dragonfly memorial is on the right side of the ridge overlooking Clatteringshaws Loch and easily missed if you are too far left. Even after all this time there is still a big scar under the memorial and the scattered debris of that fateful day in 1937; heat-fused perspex and aluminium, wiring, wood and chips of green paint. Please do not remove anything.

From the memorial continue downhill towards the forestry and follow a wall on the west (left) to where it leads down through a clearing, sometimes quite muddy, to the road. Turn left to the start.

On your return it's worth visiting Bruce's Stone at Raploch Moss on the east side of Clatteringshaws Loch where Robert the Bruce rested after putting to flight a force of 200 English at bivouac with the help of his brother Edward Bruce and Sir James Douglas in 1307. The battle marked the start of Bruce's struggle for Scottish independence and the stone is cared for by the National Trust for Scotland (see also Walk 19).

Incidentally, Clatteringshaws Loch – the name is thought to derive from the noisy clattering of the Blackwater of Dee over the glaciated rocks – was artificially enlarged into a reservoir to feed Glenlee Power Station near St John's Town of Dalry via an underground tunnel at its north-east end; part of the Galloway Water Power Scheme, which was fully operational from 1936.

Wording on the Dragonfly monument.

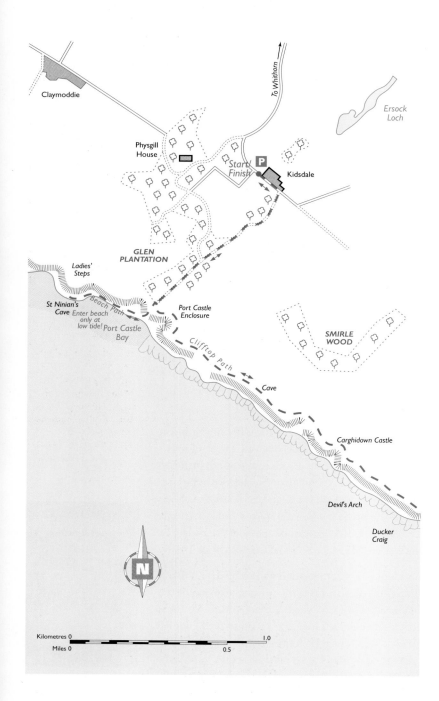

ST NINIAN'S CAVE

The crucible of Scottish Christianity seems an unlikely title for the small Galloway town of Whithorn, with its medieval streets and 18th and 19th century houses.

But it was here that Bishop Nynia, better known as St Ninian, arrived in about AD400 and established a distinctive white church, although whether the stone was white or whether it was white plastered or lime-washed isn't recorded. What is certain, however, is that Ninian's Ad Candida Casa — the White or Shining House — was the seed from which the organised Christian faith spread through Scotland.

Ninian himself is thought to have been a Roman-trained Briton (Christianity was encouraged in the Roman Empire with the accession of Constantine in

INFORMATION

Distance: 4 km (2½ miles).

Start and Finish: Kidsdale car-park. From Newton Stewart take A714 south to Wigtown then A746 through Whithorn. Turn left on A747 and in 1.5 km turn right on a minor road signposted Kidsdale. Follow it to the car park in 2 km.

Terrain: Paths and stony beach. The walk is signposted.

Map: OS Landranger sheet 83, Newton Stewart and Kirkcudbright.

Refreshments: Shops and pubs in Whithorn.

Opening hours: *Whithorn Visitor Centre* offers a range of audio-visual displays, museum and guided tours. Open Apr.-Oct., daily 1030–1730. Admission charge.

St. Ninian's Cave.

The wood through which the track leads down to the beach and St. Ninian's Cave.

AD315), and the initiative for his appointment is thought to have come from an already existing Christian community that required a bishop. St Ninian died at Whithorn in AD432.

By the late 6th century Galloway had been invaded by pagan tribes from England who became well established in south-west Scotland by 650. Speakers of Northumbrian English, Welsh and Irish were the native languages, and Christianity had re-established itself in the area with the conversion of the Northumbrian leaders in 630.

Anglian clergy dominated the church in Galloway by the mid 8th century, and at Whithorn and in the immediate area, the following 200 years saw the establishment of a monastery and a period of great devotion and cultural development. A large collection of fine stone crosses, some of the earliest Christian monuments in Scotland, have survived from that period. Many of them can be seen at Whithorn (other early stones can be seen at Kirkmadrine on Walk 24 and more stones at Dumfries museum, Walk 6). However, the finest of them all is the impressive 17-foot cross at Ruthwell near Annan, east of Dumfries (GR 100681).

Invasion by Gall-Ghaidhils, partly pagan and partly Christian from the Hebrides, Kintyre, Ireland and the Isle of Man followed the collapse of Northumbrian influence in the late 9th and early 10th centuries, and boundaries changed frequently. However by the 11th century Galloway was part of the Vikings' North Sea empire which ranged from Norway, Ireland and Greenland to eastern Ireland, Cumbria, Shetland and Orkney.

But the thread running through the centuries is Ninian's White House – Hwiterne in Anglo-Saxon (hence Whithorn) and to the Vikings, Hvitsborg.

St Ninian's cave itself lies on the coast west of Whithorn; legend has it that the saint used it as a devotional retreat and this attracted many pilgrims from all over Europe to the site. Certainly the cave has

Bluebells in the wood leading to the beach and St. Ninian's Cave.

been visited by pilgrims since the 8th century as excavations between 1883 and 1886 revealed about 11 stones and crosses dating from this period which are now in the Whithorn Priory Museum.

The cave is quite shallow and can be a little disappointing visually, although the approach and setting are splendid, so a visit to the stones in the museum and the Whithorn archaeological dig is recommended first, to fire the imagination.

Since 1986 archaeologists have been excavating the ruins of the Northumbrian monastery and the later medieval priory-cathedral that stand behind George Street, and have uncovered layers of occupation from the early Christians to the Vikings. A building at the eastern end of the crypt of the priory-cathedral could even be Ninian's Candida Casa.

To visit the cave park at Kidsdale, walk down the farm road and follow the ancient monument signs. Go down the track on the right, and then into a wood. Cross over a ford and continue down through the woods, lined with bluebells in the spring. The track then runs alongside a burn which leads out onto the beach at another signpost. The cave is quite clear up the big stony beach on the right.

On a fine day the Isle of Man can be seen quite clearly on the left and the Mull of Galloway on the right. Approaching the cave there is a short ramp on the right-hand side leading up to the cave, which has an information plaque on the wall. If further exercise is required then the beach can be followed west, taking care with the tides, or the cliffs walked eastward to Burrow Head.

If time allows, a visit can also be made to St Ninian's Chapel just east of the Isle of Whithorn, which dates from the early 1300s.

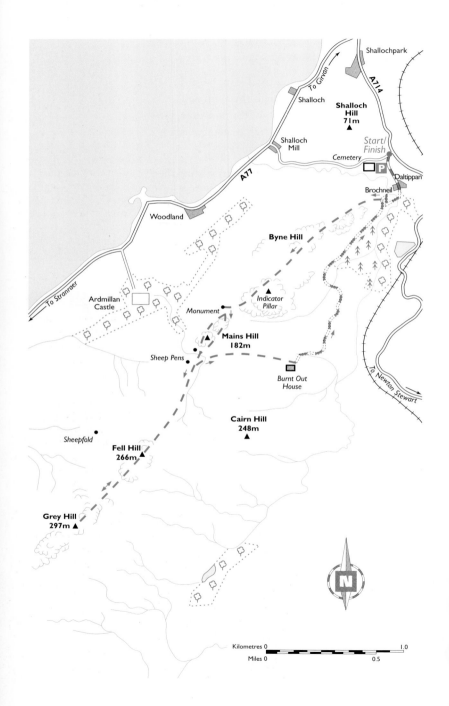

Shallochpark

A714

To Girvan

Shalloch

Shalloch
Hill
71m

Shalloch
Mill

*Start/
Finish*

A77

Cemetery

P

Daltippan

Brochneil

Woodland

Byne Hill

To Stranraer

Ardmillan
Castle

Monument

*Indicator
Pillar*

Mains Hill
182m

Sheep Pens

Burnt Out
House

To Newton Stewart

Cairn Hill
248m

Sheepfold

Fell Hill
266m

Grey Hill
297m

N

Kilometres 0   1.0

Miles 0   0.5

BYNE HILL AND GREY HILL

Girvan's claims to fame as the holiday resort of south-west Scotland are its fine sandy beach, harbour and fishing and the ever-present bulk of Ailsa Craig out at sea.

You could be forgiven for thinking this wasn't walking country – the name Byne is thought to derive from byng, meaning a heap! – but the hills to the south of the town give an excellent day's exercise through interesting scenery, with extensive views of Girvan, Arran and Northern Ireland, and on a fine day Kintyre and possibly the islands of Islay and Jura beyond.

The walk starts at the cemetery just off the A714 at the base of Byne Hill. Walk up the lane on your left towards Brochnell farm where permission should be sought for the walk. Pass through the farmyard and go through a gate which leads down to the burn and another gate. The section between the two gates is very short, but it can be very muddy and have cattle in it.

Head south-west up the hillside, which is quite steep and banded with lots of small conglomerate cliffs. From the very start the views open up quickly, with Girvan and its seafront stretched out below. A false summit is reached first and then the summit of Byne Hill, recognised by its pillar and direction indicator.

INFORMATION

Distance: 9 km (5½ miles)

Start and Finish: Beside the cemetery. From the roundabout at the south end of Girvan, go left on the A714 and the cemetery is on the right after 1 km. Please park carefully.

Terrain: Wellingtons or boots are recommended as the going can be rough and muddy. In poor weather waterproofs and a map and compass are needed.

Map: OS Landranger sheet 76, Girvan.

Refreshments: Full facilities in Girvan.

Opening hours: *The Tourist Information Centre* is on Bridge Street (call 01292 252555 for times). Toilets in the car-park.

Other Activities: Ailsa Craig is worth visiting. A boat can be hired in Girvan. *Culzean Castle and Country Park* north of Turnberry is owned by the National Trust for Scotland and gives a good day out.

Byne Hill with Ailsa Craig beyond.

Byne Hill with Grey Hill beyond it seen from just north of Girvan.

The summit of Grey Hill with its trig point can be seen away in the distance to the south-west, and this is the final objective of the walk. Drop down to the col between Byne Hill and the next little hillock; down on the right is a 6 m monument of heavily weathered sandstone facing out to sea. Various fallen blocks and the remains of a fence surround the monument which has been cemented up in places, but unfortunately there's no inscription left.

It's possible to go over the hillock or skirt it on the left via a cattle track, although it can be a bit muddy and rough. From the base of the hillock drop down past gorse to the walls of an old sheep pen and a gate where a wall turns into a fence. Cross over the gate into the bottom of a broad burn-filled gully and climb steadily until Fell Hill and Grey Hill appear ahead.

The route looks deceptively steep and impressive, but when you actually get on it, it's a lot less steep and gives a steady uphill walk. Looking back from the flanks of Fell Hill there are superb views back to Byne Hill, Girvan and the shoreline. A broad shoulder is followed in a southerly direction until Grey Hill and its trig point emerge ahead.

Continue over Fell Hill past another sheep pen, descend to the col between the two hills and then climb up to the summit of Grey Hill from where there are very fine views all around, moorland running down to fields on the east and beyond that the top of the Merrick, the coast on the west and beyond that the North Channel and Northern Ireland. To the south the coast leads round to Carleton Bay and beyond it Knockdolian Hill above Ballantrae. Further south Luce Bay and the Galloway peninsula can be seen in the distance.

Return over Fell Hill and descend the gully back down to the sheep pens. Cross over the burn and follow the fence and wall on the right, keeping to their right-hand side until a house and farm buildings appear ahead. This is part of the Scottish Wildlife Trust's Grey Hill grasslands wildlife reserve. At the time of writing the house was burnt out, but it may be refurbished in time.

Cross the stile where the fence joins the outbuildings and follow the track through the farmyard and out of the gate below. The track now leads past a stand of fine beech trees and back to the farm where you started.

The monument between Byne Hill and Grey Hill seen from the coast road.

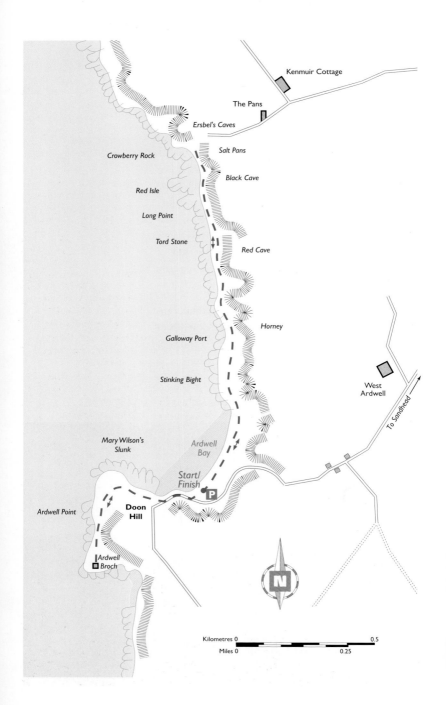

Kenmuir Cottage

The Pans

Ersbel's Caves

Salt Pans

Crowberry Rock

Black Cave

Red Isle

Long Point

Tord Stone

Red Cave

Horney

Galloway Port

Stinking Bight

West
Ardwell

To Sandhead

*Mary Wilson's
Slunk*

*Ardwell
Bay*

Start/
Finish

P

Ardwell Point

**Doon
Hill**

**Ardwell
Broch**

N

Kilometres 0   0.5

Miles 0   0.25

ARDWELL BROCH

Brochs, the circular dry-stone defensive towers, are unique to Scotland and are mostly found in coastal locations on the northern part of mainland Scotland and in the western and northern isles. Of these, perhaps the 15 m high broch at Mousa (Shetland) is the best preserved and most photographed in Scotland, while Dun Carloway on Shetland, Gurness on Orkney and those at Glenelg on the mainland opposite Skye are fine examples with walls up to 6 m still standing.

Of the 500 or so brochs recorded in Scotland only about a dozen lie outside this north-western area, including a small cluster of four round Stranraer and on the western coast of Galloway. By far the best of these is at Ardwell. Alas, the remains of Ardwell cannot compete with its northern cousins, but enough can be seen to imagine the tower that must have dominated this section of the coast.

Similar in look to the tapered profile of a modern cooling tower, brochs were designed as defensive community homesteads around the turn of the pre-Christian and Christian eras, about 100BC to AD200. They are characterised by an easily defended single entrance and thick and high double-skinned walls containing rooms and a staircase to the upper levels.

The remains of Ardwell Broch are well situated on a small spit of land jutting into the sea.

INFORMATION

Distance: 7 km (4½ miles) including Ardwell Bay beach. From Stranraer take A716 south, or from A75 just west of Glenluce take A715 which joins A716 just north of Sandhead. Continue through Sandhead and then turn right on a minor road (signed for the Kirkmadrine Stones, Clachanmore and High Ardwell). At the end of the minor road, continue down the rough track to the fine sandy beach of Ardwell Bay and a large well-maintained car-park.

Start and Finish: Ardwell Bay car-park

Terrain: Easy, fields, sand and shingle.

Map: OS Landranger sheet 82, Stranraer and Glen Luce

Refreshments: Sandhead is the nearest town.

Opening hours: The Tourist Information Centre on Bridge Street, Stranraer is open all year round (call 01776 702595 for times).

Other Activities: For the green-fingered, the balmy climate of Galloway makes for beautiful gardens. Public gardens can be found at the nearby Ardwell House, Port Logan Botanic Garden and Castle Kennedy Gardens east of Stranraer. The ruins of Glenluce Abbey to the south-east of Stranraer are also worth visiting.

Archaeologists have suggested a roofed timber gallery may have existed inside some brochs.

One final interesting fact is that Scotland's brochs show a remarkable degree of uniformity in design and structure and it has been suggested, quite sensibly, that they could have been built by a class of professional broch makers who hired out their services. This might account for some of the brochs in Southern Scotland, possibly paid for by chieftains and communities seeking protection from the invading Roman armies.

From the car-park, the broch is a short walk along the coast to the south. Leave the car-park and continue on the track to a gate. Go through the gate, cross a field and then walk above the coast to a stile from where the broch can be seen as a large pile of stones on a spit of land pointing out into the sea. If the field is filled with livestock, it may be necessary to go round it by skirting the fence and rocks to the right of the first gate and then walking along the rocky, and unfortunately junk-ridden sea shore.

The cliff top path with the large pile of stones marking Ardwell Broch on the right.

On closer inspection a number of sections of the broch's walls can be seen quite easily as can two 'rooms' between the inner and outer. The walls are about 4m in total thickness and about 2m at their highest point. Unusually, the broch has a landward and seaward entrance, the latter being a very rare feature.

One further reason for brochs in this area is that the sedimentary greywacke rock naturally breaks into long

Fishing from the rocks is a
popular activity in the area.

flat stones, excellent for dry-stone building. The same
is true of the sandstone in Orkney and Caithness (red
Caithness flagstones are famous), where some of the
highest concentrations of brochs are found.

From the broch it is possible to continue a short way
along a coastal path to the south, the low rocks are
often frequented by fishermen, but fences soon get in
the way.

If you wish more exercise then it is better to return to
Ardwell Bay, from where it is possible to have a 6 km
walk north along the beach to the small cottage at Salt
Pans and back. Depending on the state of the tide the
walk will be on sand or shingle.

On your return to the main road at Sandhead it is well
worth making a short diversion to see the Kirkmadrine
Stones. The stones are the oldest Christian
monuments in Scotland outside Whithorn (see Walk
22) and are on permanent display in a glass-fronted
cabinet in the porch of Kirkmadrine Church, reached
by a short walk up a tree-lined track from the road.

Two of the gravestones date from AD400 to AD500 and
have Latin inscriptions naming the priests they
commemorate. One other is from about AD600 and
there are other fragments of crosses dating from the
8th and 12th centuries. The three oldest stones were
discovered in the 19th century being used as gateposts
and a stile slab in a nearby wall, and mark the area as
an important early Christian cemetery.

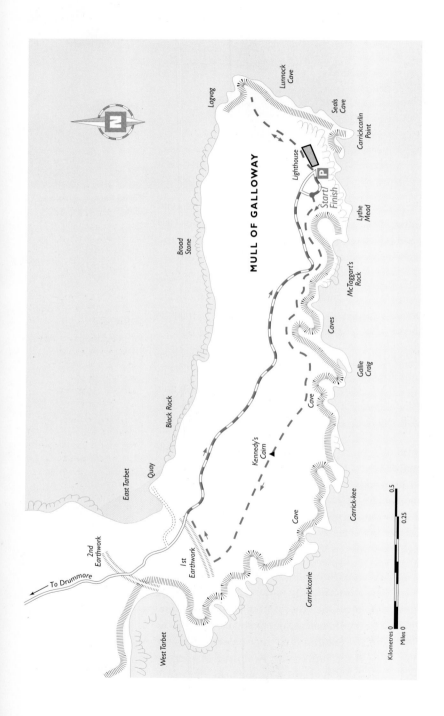

MULL OF GALLOWAY

Lunnock Cave

Logvag

Seals Cave

Carrickcarlin Point

Lighthouse

P

Start/ Finish

Lythe Mead

Broad Stone

McTaggart's Rock

Caves

Gallie Craig

Black Rock

Cave

Kennedy's Cairn

East Tarbet

Quay

Cave

Carrick-kee

2nd Earthwork

1st Earthwork

Carrickcorie

To Drummore

West Tarbet

Kilometres 0   0.5

Miles 0   0.25

MULL OF GALLOWAY

Scotland's most southerly point is a grassy windswept headland at the tip of the Rhins of Galloway, the peninsula that juts out below Stranraer. At the height of a winter storm the Mull of Galloway is a wild, foreboding place – mull derives from the Gaelic word maol meaning bare or bal, and is a word commonly used to describe headland – but for the rest of the year, the varied seabirds and wild flowers, views and impressive cliff landscape make it worth a visit.

Unlike the other walks in this book there are no distinctive 'routes' to be followed at the Mull and that is part of its charm. However, anyone wanting exercise will find this extensive and hilly headland gives excellent walking.

The focus of attention for anyone visiting the Mull is the walled lighthouse at the highest and most south-easterly point. The 19 m lighthouse was built in 1828 by Robert Stevenson to mark the western boundary of the Solway Firth and to guide ships away from the cliffs and strong tidal race round the Mull, while travelling north to Loch Ryan, the North Channel and the Firth of Clyde. The light was first lit in 1830. Stevenson was engineer to the Northern Lighthouse Board for 47 years and designed 23 lighthouses. His grandson was the famous author Robert Louis Stevenson.

INFORMATION

Distance: 4 km (2½ miles).

Start and Finish: Mull of Galloway lighthouse car-park. From Stranraer take A716 south, or from Glenluce on A75 take A715 until it meets A716. Continue on A716 to Drummore, then take B7041. At its end take the left fork and continue to the car-park at the Mull.

Terrain: Paths and grass.

Map: OS Landranger sheet 82, Stranraer and Glen Luce.

Refreshments: There is usually a mobile snack bar in the car-park during the summer. Drummore has shops and pubs.

Opening hours: The Information Centre in Mill Street, Drummore, is run on a voluntary basis and is normally open Apr.-Sept. (no telephone).

The spectacular cliffs on the southside of the Mull, below the lighthouse.

Mull of Galloway lighthouse.

As you would expect, the Mull's steep broken cliffs teem with birdlife all year round and part of the area is managed by the Royal Society for the Protection of Birds as the Mull of Galloway Nature Reserve.

To the east of the lighthouse is the first part of the headland worth exploring. From the car-park go through the pedestrian gate in the wall surrounding the lighthouse precinct. Unlike the rest of the Mull which is grazed and manured by cattle, this area is untouched by animals and is covered with heather.

Follow the path past the buildings and a row of cottages aiming for the furthest part of the headland. Descend carefully down the path – this is no place to slip – until you can look down and back to view birds nesting on the cliffs, riding the swell and diving for fish. Guillemot, kittiwake, herring gull, shag and fulmar are all present, while black guillemot, razorbill, cormorant, greater and lesser black-backed gull and gannets from the nearby Scares rocks can also be seen. If you are lucky you may even see some puffins. During the nesting season the air is filled with screeching birds and the pungent odour of guano.

It is possible to descend on a path right down to the sea, but considerable care must be taken. The earth path is slippery and a fall onto the rocks or into the sea would be very serious and most probably fatal. From above, the fast flowing currents of the tidal race round the Mull can be seen quite clearly. As well as birds the area has a wide variety of wild flowers including sea campion, yellow vetch, and mountain milk-vetch.

Returning to the car-park, it is worth admiring the view. On a good day the coast of Northern Ireland can be seen quite clearly to the west. The Isle of Man lurks away to the south and closer, off to the east, are the spiked tops of the Big and Little Scares in Luce Bay. Behind the Scares is Burrow Head and the coast at St Ninian's Cave (Walk 22). Towering above everything in the distance are Cairnsmore of Fleet (Walk 15) and to its left in the distance, Merrick (Walk 18).

Return to the lighthouse car-park. If you are lucky the mobile snack bar will be there and you can have a cup of tea or an ice cream, depending on the weather.

The next walk takes you round the southern cliffs towards the prominent Kennedy's Cairn atop the small hill to the west. The walking here is on springy close-cropped grass and very pleasant. From the car-park follow the cliff top towards the cairn, descending at first to skirt round the cliffs and then rising slowly towards the cairn. At this point it's worth looking back at the fine cliff scenery below the lighthouse, hidden from above.

The cairn is soon reached and can be climbed quite easily for a panorama of rolling fields, white painted farmhouses and the gentle eastern coastline leading to Cailiness Point. The cairn also gives a good overall view of the double line of earthworks that cross from coast to coast at the isthmus. The northern line runs from south of the bay at West Tarbet to north of the bay at East Tarbet; about 300 m to the south the better preserved of the two earthworks runs for about 400 m from a point south of West Tarbet to south of the bay at East Tarbet.

It is worth descending from the cairn to explore the southern earthwork at close quarters as it is difficult to stop the car here on the return journey. The earthwork is made up of three ditches with two substantial banks about 4 m wide and 2 m high, with four entrances, although these have been blocked by a later turf wall on top.

Looking down on the cliffs below the tip of the Mull – a mass of birds and wild flowers.

The origins of these earthworks are unknown, although they are thought to date from the Iron Age, about 1000BC. The earthworks are almost certainly defensive in nature, but no further evidence has been found of other fortifications. If the Mull was an Iron Age fortress then it would be one of the largest in Britain.

From here two return routes are possible. Either follow the road back to the car-park or cross to the northern coast and follow this back to the car.

INDEX

Other titles in this series:

Cycling guides: